FEAST FOR LIFE

LINDA PROVUS BARTLETT AND GRETCHEN SANDIN JORDAN

DESIGN BY THIRST · PHOTOGRAPHY BY TIM TURNER

CollinsPublishersSanFrancisco
A Division of HarperCollins*Publishers*

ADDITIONAL PHOTO CREDITS

Page 25: Lou Manna; 26: Claude Alexandre; 28: Stuart Rogers, Ltd; 30: George Lange; 32: Patrice Meigneux; 38: Donn Young;

39: Stewart Ferebee; 45: Annie Leibovitz; 48: Blake Little; 59: Michael Baz; 61: Courtesy of *Winds;* 62: Will Mosgrove; 66: Troy House;

67: Greg Gorman; 69: Warren Jagger. MR. POTATO HEAD® is a trademark of Hasbro, Inc. ©1996 Hasbro, Inc. All Rights Reserved.

Used with permission; 72: Heidi Gibbs; 78: Julian Broad; 80: Photo of Lidia Bastianich and her husband Felice by Gianni Renna;

82: Harry Langdon; 84: David Montgomery; 85: Firooz Zahedi; 88: Dick Zimmerman; 90: J. M. Collignon; 92: Tabitha King; 95: Mike Laye;

97: Aloma Ichinose; 106: Marcel Erhard; 107: Jaime Ardiles-Arce; 108: Walter Iooss; 110: M. Deval; 112: Greg Gorman; 118: Chris Haston;

119: Ellen von Unwerth; 123: Neil Barr; 124: Luca Vignelli; 135: Mario Casilli. Reprinted with permission from *TV Guide.* 1995 Copyright,

News America Publications, Inc. (*TV Guide* Magazine); 140: Dana Fineman; 141: Michael Jacobs; 143: Peter Nash; 148: Todd Gray;

150: Kingmond Young; 160: Jean-Louis Blochlaine; 163: Jonathan Exley; 167: Karl Lagerfeld; 169: Robert Battishini; 170: Phillip Merle;

171: Francis Clement; 174: Sarah Moon; 178: Ken Regan; 182: Alberto Tolot; 184: Paul Elledge.

RECIPES REPRINTED WITH THE PERMISSION OF THE AUTHORS

Page 22: *Harry's Bar Cookbook,* Bantam Books, 1988; 25: *Cooking with David Burke,* Knopf, 1994; 33: *Joachim Splichal's Patina Cookbook,*

Collins San Francisco, 1995; 38: *Becoming a Chef,* Van Nostrand Reinhold, 1993; 39: *Martha Stewart's Quick Cook Menus,*

Clarkson Potter Publishers, 1992; 63: *Randy Travis' Favorite Recipes,* Cookbook Pubs., 1989; 73: *Vincent's Cookbook,* Ten Speed Press, 1994;

82: *Adventures in the Kitchen,* Random House, 1991; 84: *Country Color,* Rizzoli International Publications, USA; 91: *Regional French Cooking,*

Flammarion; 101: *Cooking with Daniel Boulud,* Random House, 1993; 106: *Eurodélices,* S.A. Éditions Consulaires; 123: *Entertaining with Kathie Lee*

and Regis: Year Round Holiday Recipes, Entertaining Tips, and Party Ideas, by Regis Philbin & Kathie Lee Gifford with Barbara Albright.

Copyright © 1994, Regis Philbin and Lambchop Productions. Reprinted with permission by Hyperion; 150: *The Enlightened Cuisine,*

Macmillan, 1985; 162: *French Food: American Accent,* Clarkson Potter Publishers, 1996; 165: *Lakers Charity Cookbook;* Taylor Publishing Co., 1985;

175: *Pillsbury's The Complete Book of Baking,* Viking-Penguin, 1993.

First published 1996 by Collins Publishers San Francisco
1160 Battery Street, San Francisco, California 94111
HarperCollins Web Site: http://www.harpercollins.com

Library of Congress Cataloging-in-Publication Data:

Bartlett, Linda Provus
        Feast for life / Linda Provus Bartlett, Gretchen Sandin Jordan ;
        design by Thirst ; photography by Tim Turner.
        p.   cm.
        Includes index
        ISBN 0-00-255459-3
        1. Cookery. 2. Celebrities. I. Jordan, Gretchen Sandin. II. Title.
TX714.B3723   1996
641.5 – dc20   95-53805

Printed in Hong Kong
DNP 10 9 8 7 6 5 4 3 2 1

DEDICATION

WE DEDICATE THIS BOOK
TO THE COURAGEOUS
MEN, WOMEN, AND CHILDREN
WHO ARE HIV POSITIVE
OR LIVING WITH AIDS.
AND ALSO TO OUR DEAR FRIENDS
WHO ARE NO LONGER WITH US.
THE MEMORIES WE HAVE OF YOU
WILL FOREVER LIVE
IN OUR HEARTS.

table of contents

foreword

"From the bottom of my heart, I want to thank each and every one

of my friends and colleagues in the entertainment, design,

and sports communities for sharing recipes and memories for this

wonderful cookbook. By your willingness to confront this terrible tragedy with

your time and support, you have proven that we are truly a human race.

You have proven that we are able to put aside our differences for

a common good and love one another with sensitivity and compassion.

I particularly would like to thank Linda and Gretchen for their untiring

devotion to the AIDS *crisis, and for the leadership they provide in furthering*

education and understanding.

Most of all, I would like to thank you, the reader, for supporting our efforts

to improve the lives of millions. I call upon each of you to continually prove

that our love outweighs our need to hate, that our compassion is more compelling

than our need to blame, that our sensitivity to those in need is stronger than

our greed, that our ability to reason overcomes our fear, and that at the end

of each of our lives, we can look back and be proud that we have treated others

with the kindness, dignity, and respect that every human being deserves.

God bless."

ELIZABETH TAYLOR

acknowledgements

Our deepest gratitude to the chefs and celebrities who have so generously shared their recipes and heartfelt memories to make this book possible. We are especially indebted to Elizabeth Taylor for her invaluable support throughout the project and her generosity in contributing the foreword to our cookbook.

· · · · · · · · · · · · · ·

It is difficult finding the words to express our gratitude to image designer Rick Valicenti of Thirst. He has shared with us his unique perspective on life, engaging wit, and incredible talent, to design a cookbook like no other. To Rick, we are eternally grateful. To Chester, typographist, a true Renaissance man, we thank you for crossing the Atlantic for us and offering your wellspring of creativity. Our wholehearted thanks to project administrator Barbara Valicenti for her endless encouragement and keen organizational skills, which helped to keep everyone on the same page. Thanks also to Patricking who augmented the Thirst vision, and to Wm Valicenti for his additional photographic contributions. We gratefully acknowledge the following illustrators, who have shared their vast talent and magical sense of humor with us: Barry Blitt, Victor Juhasz, Stephen Kroninger, Mercedes McDonald, Lynn Rowe Reed, Ed Schweitzer, James Noel Smith, William Spring, Mark Ulriksen, and Kirsten Ulve.

· · · · · · · · · · · · · ·

We are indebted to Tim Turner. His immense talent gave us the beautiful food and background photographs that appear throughout the book. Many thanks for his invaluable guidance, patience, and encouragement throughout the project. Special thanks to Lynn Gagné and Maria Kernahan for their painstaking effort in styling the food in our photographs. Thank you to Renée Miller, prop stylist, whose tireless efforts helped produce the perfect shots. To Tim's outstanding crew—Rod LaFleur, Steve Oatley and Dan Schrock—a million thanks. We would also like to thank Gamma Photo Labs for processing, Calumet Photographic for photo supplies, and the Prop Room Inc. for props.

· · · · · · · · · · · · · ·

To our friend Patrick Chabert, the sous chef at Le Français, whose expertise and incredible knowledge of the culinary world he so generously shared. Thank you Patrick, for your tireless effort in recruiting so many of the great chefs within the covers of our book and for your total commitment to our project. We will always be grateful.

· · · · · · · · · · · · · ·

We would like to thank most affectionately our incredible agent, Phyllis Wender, who took a huge leap of faith hooking up with two first-time authors. Her warmth, support, and constant encouragement mean a great deal.

· · · · · · · · · · · · · ·

Deep appreciation to our editor at Collins Publishers, Meesha Halm, for understanding our vision and believing in our project. Her advice and guidance throughout were invaluable. We'd also like to thank Jenny Collins, the production editor, who offered us her incredible patience and insight during the long hours of editing. Thanks to Terri Driscoll for her design input. To our friend, Michael Cerre, who saw the great potential in our project and urged us to reach for the stars, we will always be grateful.

· · · · · · · · · · · · · ·

Thanks to our guardian angel Geoff Blain, with whom we share a common bond. His friendship, unstinting help, and belief in our project will always be treasured.

· · · · · · · · · · · · · ·

We will forever be indebted to Martha Nelson, editor of *In-Style* magazine and her team: Carrie Tuhy, senior editor; Hope Hening, marketing director; and Mary Jane Skarren, Martha Nelson's assistant, for their show of faith and confidence in us and our cookbook.

· · · · · · · · · · · · · ·

We will always be grateful to Barry Bluestein and Kevin Morrisey for generously sharing their knowledge of the cookbook business and helping us in the early stages of development with our writing style.

· · · · · · · · · · · · · ·

Our special thanks to David Sheppard, Executive Director of DIFFA, for his warmth and support on our project. And to our friend Brian Hurst, who generously shared his knowledge of contacting celebrities, many thanks.

· · · · · · · · · · · · · ·

We would like to thank Theresa and Warren Littlefield for so generously sharing their family recipe with us and helping us obtain several additional recipes from their NBC family.

· · · · · · · · · · · · · ·

To Michael Hasten, Robert Denvir, and Dennis Kelly of the Winston and Strawn law firm in Chicago, our deepest gratitude for their legal expertise and knowledgeable help in structuring the Feast for Life Foundation. A heartfelt thank you to Michael Shain of Wineberg & Lewis, C.P.A.'s, for so generously contributing his accounting skills on behalf of the foundation.

· · · · · · · · · · · · · ·

We wish we had more room to adequately thank all of the people who selflessly gave of their time to help make this book a reality. We hope that by seeing their names on this page, they will realize how much they mean to us. Once again, thank you to Robert Acker, Lynn Anderson, André and Heather Backar, Jon Bernstein, Laurel Reed Caputo, Joyce Coombs, Ian Cumming, Bobbi Dell'Aquilo, Michelle Edwards, Jodi Hennifield, Robert Isabell, Silvia Mannix, Libby Matlin, Rachel McLish, Suzanne Maguire, Melanie Morris, Julie Parker, Charlie Romanoff, Patti Rubin, Tracy Taylor, Joan Weinstein, and Harvey Wineberg.

FROM the HEART

My love and affection to my 15-year-old son, Chris, who was indispensable in evaluating
the dessert recipes; he was particularly thorough with the brownies. To my 19-year-old daughter,
Courtney, who was a sophomore in high school when she started helping us with this project,
I love you and thank you for all the work you did with such enthusiasm and energy.
My heartfelt thanks to my parents, Judith and Edwin Provus, who taught me the importance
of humor and tenacity when trying to accomplish a goal. And to my husband and soul mate Barry,
my thanks and deepest love for always being there to help me when I needed it.
Your sensitivity, selflessness, and unconditional love, have enabled me to pursue
and accomplish that which I thought was beyond my reach.

LINDA PROVUS BARTLETT

We offer no recipe in this cookbook for sweet-potato pie, but I've got one and her name is
Colby Elizabeth. She is my three-year-old daughter, who has spent more time in the kitchen
than she has on the playground…thanks for being you. My love and thanks to Jenny and JW
who were assigned the delightful culinary duty of taste-testing almost every recipe in the book
and loved each bite! Thank you to my parents, Helen and Richard Sandin, for their support,
encouragement, and love in all endeavors upon which I set my sights. And finally, to my
best friend, my loving husband Jay, who has urged me to pursue my dreams and has helped
make them all come true.

GRETCHEN SANDIN JORDAN

introduction

Which foods do celebrities eat when they step out of the limelight and into the privacy of their own homes? We asked over one hundred celebrities and world-renowned chefs for special recipes that have personal significance to them; what we got in return were not only directions for wonderful, original cuisine, but also intimate glimpses into the lives and traditions of our contributors. These dishes serve up memories of romantic encounters, personal triumphs, cherished family rituals, and sun-soaked days of childhood.

Why were so many famous people willing to share such personal associations? The answer is simple: *A good cause.*

All of the authors' proceeds for this book will be donated to the Pediatric AIDS Foundation in Los Angeles and the Design Industries Foundation Fighting AIDS/Chicago. The Pediatric AIDS Foundation dispenses research grant money in the fight against AIDS, and DIFFA/Chicago supports agencies that provide services for men, women, and children living with HIV and AIDS. In this way, the book will contribute to a genuine feast for life.

We came to this project with more than our love of cooking. While Gretchen holds a culinary degree from the Cooking Hospitality Institute of Chicago, and Linda loves to concoct dishes from her huge cookbook collection, between the two of us we have been active in raising money for AIDS for over a decade. The idea of compiling a cookbook that combined our interests had intrigued us for quite a while. Finally we decided to produce a book that offered not only good eating but also good reading and, above all, sustenance to those in need.

First we wrote out a celebrity wish list and started drawing on people's generosity. We compiled a packet explaining our project; we asked for an original recipe of personal significance. We explained that no one need be an accomplished cook in order to participate; the recipes could include simple family favorites, such as Mother's decadent fudge brownies that she made every New Year's Eve or Grandfather's spicy barbecue sauce that was slathered over ribs on hot summer nights. What we were after was good food and fond memories.

In pursuing recipes, we left no opportunity unexplored.
One summer day in 1992, on a boat bound for Capri, Linda and another woman
fell into conversation. A Londoner, the woman agreed to drop off
Feast for Life requests on the doorsteps of Margaret Thatcher and Jeffrey Archer.
Both leaders contributed recipes: Baroness Thatcher's Pasta with
Pork and Basil, and Lord Archer's Smoked Chicken Salad.
When Gretchen was exercising at a health club on Long Island,
she spotted Calvin Klein and Martha Stewart.
Although hot and sweaty, she didn't hesitate to make her pitch.
The result: two more contributions, Klein's Grilled Jumbo Shrimp
with Fresh Lemon Juice and Garlic, and Stewart's Carrot
and Parsnip Soup with Coriander.

In the process, we came to know our contributors a little better.
Tracy Austin broke training for Sour Cream Coffee Cake. Regis Philbin sent us
his wife Joy's fabulous Chicken with Mustard Sauce, a low-fat dish invented
to vary the menu after Regis suffered a blocked artery. And we found recipes
for every level of cook, from Dave Barry's Toast with Peanut Butter
to French chef Daniel Boulud's Short Ribs Miroton.
Some dishes have already started creating traditions of their own
in our extended families. Gretchen bakes Tracy Austin's
Coffee Cake whenever she has unexpected guests drop by.
Warren Littlefield's Chicken Cacciatore has become a weekly ritual
at the Bartlett household.

Many people have taken our efforts — and our cause — to their hearts
to make this cookbook a reality. Numerous acclaimed chefs have joined dozens
of celebrities in contributing their favorite recipes and the personal stories
behind them to create this one-of-a-kind collection.

We hope that *Feast for Life* will create wonderful memories for you.
May it enrich your life, just as you are enriching the lives of so many
through your support.

APPETIZERS & HORS D'ŒUVRES

Marlee Matlin

SPINACH AND ARTICHOKE HEART DIP

One 14-ounce can artichoke hearts,
drained and chopped
One 10-ounce package
frozen spinach, thawed,
drained, and chopped
2 tablespoons mayonnaise
½ cup (2 ounces) shredded
Monterey Jack cheese
Salt and ground white pepper to taste
½ cup (2 ounces) grated
Parmesan cheese

SERVES

4

preparation

Preheat the oven to 350 degrees F. In a large bowl, combine the artichoke hearts, spinach, mayonnaise, and ¼ cup of the Monterey Jack cheese. Season with salt and pepper. Stir until well blended.

. . . .

Pour the spinach mixture into an 8–inch round baking dish. Sprinkle the Parmesan and remaining jack cheese on top and bake in the oven for 20 minutes, or until bubbly.

. . . .

Remove the dip from the oven and serve immediately with chips, crackers, or bread.

WHEN MY SISTER-IN-LAW, KIM MACIAS, FIRST CAME
TO MY HOME, SHE TOLD ME SHE COULD COOK.
I REALLY DIDN'T BELIEVE HER BECAUSE SHE'S
TWO YEARS YOUNGER THAN ME. WHEN SHE MADE
THIS ARTICHOKE-SPINACH DIP, I FELL IN LOVE
WITH IT. I'M SO LUCKY SHE'S MY SISTER-IN-LAW.
NOW SHE SHOWS ME HOW TO COOK.

preparation

Diane Sawyer

To make the dip, combine the garlic, scallions, and parsley in a food processor fitted with a steel blade, or a blender. Pulse 3 times. Add the sour cream and mayonnaise. Process until smooth. Add the Worcestershire sauce, salt, and white pepper. Process for 10 seconds. Transfer to a small serving bowl, cover, and refrigerate for at least 3 hours or, preferably, overnight.

. . . .

Preheat the oven to 450 degrees F. Grease two 15½×10½-inch sided baking sheets. Using a paring knife, follow the shape of the potatoes, and cut long, thin layers of flesh (leaving the skins on), resulting in strips approximately ½-inch wide. Repeat until all sides of the potatoes are cut away. Put the peeled, whole potatoes in a container filled with cold water, cover, and reserve for another use.

. . . .

Place the strips, skin-side up, on the prepared pans. Bake in the oven for 20 to 30 minutes, or until the potato skins are crisp and golden brown. Immediately sprinkle with the sea salt and transfer to a wire rack to cool slightly.

. . . .

Arrange the potato skins on a serving plate and serve with the scallion dip.

Editor's note: The potato skins can be made up to 1 day in advance, kept in an airtight container, and served at room temperature or reheated in a preheated 450 degree F oven for 5 minutes, or until they are warm. The dip can be made up to 3 days in advance and kept covered in the refrigerator.

ROASTED POTATO SKINS
WITH
SCALLION DIP

Scallion Dip

1 garlic clove, chopped

¼ cup chopped scallions

½ cup chopped fresh parsley

½ cup sour cream

½ cup mayonnaise

1 teaspoon Worcestershire sauce

Salt and ground white pepper to taste

Potato Skins

4 pounds Idaho baking potatoes

Sea salt to taste

SERVES

6

David Letterman

NACHOS
IMPERIALES
ESPECIAL
DE DAVID
—
One 10-ounce bag of tortilla chips
One 11-ounce jar of salsa
SERVES
1–6

preparation

Dip chips in salsa to taste.

finest Indiana's recipe

Top 10 reasons why DAVID LETTERMAN wouldn't send us a photo

10. Protesting because I wasn't allowed to submit the 'big-ass ham' recipe.

9. By not sending a picture, you've come up with this fake Top 10 list.

8. First try my recipe, then tell me if you still want a photo.

7. Photomat lost the film, and, I don't mind saying, all of my future business.

6. Don't want kidnappers to know what I look like.

5. If I give you a picture, I have nothing to give to my mom for her birthday.

4. My face and food just don't mix.

3. Just put in JFK Jr's photo, as we look very much alike.

2. Yeah, first you want a picture, and then you end up coming to my house.

1. Afraid people will fill in my gap tooth.

Jay Leno

preparation

Preheat the broiler. Rinse the chicken and pat dry with paper towels. Cut off the wing tips. Place the chicken on a broiler pan and broil for 6 minutes on each side, or until the wings are cooked through and golden brown. Remove the chicken from the oven and transfer to a serving bowl. Cover with aluminum foil to keep warm.

. . . .

In a medium saucepan, heat the olive oil over medium heat. Add the garlic and sauté for 15 seconds. Pass the tomatoes through a sieve into the saucepan. Use the bottom of a sturdy ladle to force as much of the liquid through the strainer as possible. Add the salt and garlic powder. Reduce heat to low and simmer, covered, for 20 minutes. Add the hot sauce and parsley. Continue to simmer the sauce for 3 to 4 minutes.

. . . .

Add half of the sauce to the bowl of chicken wings and stir gently with a wooden spoon to coat. Put the remaining sauce in a small bowl and use it as a dip for the wings. Serve immediately.

Editor's note: You can deep-fry the chicken wings instead of broiling them. Simply fry them according to your favorite recipe.

UNCLE LOUIE'S CHICKEN WINGS MARINARA

5 pounds chicken wings
2 tablespoons olive oil
1 garlic clove, minced
One 12-ounce can plum tomatoes, drained
Salt to taste
¼ teaspoon garlic powder
2 tablespoons Durkee's hot sauce, or to taste
1 tablespoon minced fresh parsley

MAKES ABOUT 35 WINGS

SERVES

6

Arrigo Cipriani

The most popular dish served at *Harry's Bar* in Venice is carpaccio. A dish invented by my father in 1950 and named for **Vittore Carpaccio**, the Venetian Renaissance painter, carpaccio is made by covering a plate with the **thinnest** p o s s i b l e slices of raw beef and garnishing them with shaved cheese or an olive oil dressing. To finish the dish, a cream-colored mayonnaise sauce is d r i z z l e d over the meat in a crisscross pattern.

CARPACCIO WITH SAUCE

Carpaccio

1½ pounds boned and trimmed shell of beef

Mayonnaise

1 large egg yolk at room temperature

1 teaspoon white or red wine vinegar

⅛ teaspoon dry mustard

Salt and ground white pepper to taste

¾ cup olive oil

Fresh lemon juice to taste

Sauce

¾ cup homemade mayonnaise (see above)

1 to 2 teaspoons Worcestershire sauce

1 teaspoon fresh lemon juice

2 to 3 teaspoons milk

Salt and ground white pepper to taste

Parmesan cheese

SERVES

6

preparation

To prepare the carpaccio, use a razor-sharp knife to trim all the fat, gristle, and sinew from the boned shell. Transfer the meat to the refrigerator and chill for 3 hours.

· · · · · · · · · · · · · · ·

To make the mayonnaise, combine the egg yolk, vinegar, and mustard in a small bowl. Whisk the mixture until it is well blended. Season with salt and white pepper. While beating constantly, add ½ cup of the oil, a few drops at a time. Continue whisking the mixture while adding the remaining ¼ cup oil in a thin stream to make a thick sauce, an emulsion. Season with more salt and pepper if needed, and with lemon juice. Whisk to combine.

· · · · · · · · · · · · · · ·

To make the sauce, place the mayonnaise in a small bowl. Whisk in the Worcestershire sauce and lemon juice. Whisk in enough milk to make a thin sauce that coats the back of a spoon. Season with salt and white pepper. Adjust the seasoning by adding Worcestershire sauce and/or lemon juice if necessary. Set aside.

· · · · · · · · · · · · · · ·

Place the meat on a cutting board. Using the same razor-sharp knife as before, slice the meat paper thin. Arrange the slices of meat to completely cover each of 6 salad plates. Drizzle the sauce decoratively over the meat in a crisscross pattern, shave fresh Parmesan cheese over the top, and serve immediately.

Sybille Pump

preparation

Preheat the oven to 350 degrees F. Rinse the chicken and pat it dry with paper towels. Arrange the chicken in a roasting pan large enough to hold all the pieces (layering is fine).

· · · · · · · · · · · · · ·

In a food processor fitted with a steel blade, or a blender, combine the ginger and garlic. Pulse 3 times. Add the onion, soy sauce, and honey. Process for 15 seconds. Pour the sauce over the chicken. Cover with aluminum foil and bake in the oven for 2 hours. Discard the foil and bake 45 minutes longer, or until the chicken is golden brown.

· · · · · · · · · · · · · ·

Transfer the chicken to a large serving platter. Garnish with the chopped scallions and serve.

Editor's note: You can make this dish up to 3 days in advance and store it in the refrigerator.

About 45 minutes before serving, preheat the oven to 350 degrees F. Remove the pan from the refrigerator, uncover the chicken, and let it sit at room temperature for 15 minutes. Bake in the oven for 25 to 30 minutes until warm. Remove the chicken from the oven and serve.

GINGER CHICKEN

6 pounds chicken breasts, drumsticks, thighs, and wings

½ cup coarsely chopped peeled fresh ginger

¼ cup minced garlic

1 medium onion, coarsely chopped

¾ cup soy sauce

1 cup honey

½ cup chopped scallions, including the green tops

SERVES

12

THIS UNFORGETTABLE CHICKEN DISH HAS BEEN SERVED FOR FOURTEEN YEARS AT OUR STORE, LOAVES AND FISHES, AS WELL AS AT MULTIPLE GATHERINGS MY MOTHER, ANNA, AND I HAVE CATERED. NOT ONLY IS THE MEAT SO MOIST AND TENDER THAT IT FALLS FROM THE BONE AND MELTS IN YOUR MOUTH, BUT THERE IS SOMETHING VERY SOUL-SATISFYING ABOUT THE DISH. TRY IT FOR YOURSELF AND YOUR GUESTS. IT'S SO EASY TO MAKE!

David Burke

preparation

Lightly brush the insides of ten 2×2-inch pastry rings with 1 tablespoon of the olive oil. Cover a baking sheet with waxed paper and arrange the rings in a single layer on top. Set aside.

....

In a medium bowl, using an electric mixer set at the highest speed, whip the crème fraîche until thick, stiff peaks form. Cover and refrigerate.

....

In a small saucepan, heat the remaining 4 tablespoons of olive oil over medium heat. Add the shallots and sauté until translucent, about 2 minutes. Transfer the shallots to a small bowl and add the capers, lemon zest, soy sauce, horseradish, coriander, and chervil. Mix until well blended. Divide the shallot mixture into 2 equal parts and place in 2 small bowls. Add the diced tuna to one bowl and the ground salmon to the other bowl. Add 1 teaspoon of the salt and 1 teaspoon of the white pepper to each of the bowls. Mix all the ingredients in each bowl until they are well combined.

....

Place 2 tablespoons of the tuna mixture in each of the prepared pastry rings and smooth the mixture with the back of a spoon. Place 2 tablespoons of the salmon mixture on top of the tuna mixture and smooth with the back of a spoon. Spoon 2 tablespoons of the caviar on top of the salmon, smoothing with the back of a spoon. Finish with 2 tablespoons of crème fraîche and smooth with the blade of a flat knife, making sure that

the crème fraîche is level with the top of the molds. The molds should have 4 equal layers. Transfer the baking sheet with the parfaits to the refrigerator and chill for 2 to 3 hours.

....

Remove the parfaits from the refrigerator and place each ring on an individual salad plate. Gently remove the ring, leaving the parfait on the plate. Arrange 3 toast points around each parfait and serve immediately.

This is one of my favorite dishes. It offers a counterpoint of flavors, and the presentation delights the eye. The parfaits are made of layers of salmon and tuna tartare and caviar and finished with crème fraîche. I use osetra caviar, because the flavor is more intense than beluga and plays well against the pungency of the fish tartare. Salmon caviar can also be dotted between the layers. To form the parfaits you will need pastry rings that are approximately 2 inches high and 2 inches in diameter. Two-inch pastry rings are available in gourmet shops or restaurant supply stores. When I devised this dish, I went to a hardware store that specialized in construction material, and I had them cut steel pipes into 2-inch rings.

However, any circular object can be used, including bracelets, cookie cutters, biscuit cutters, and pancake rings. The parfaits can also be prepared in ramekins or demitasse cups, but you won't have the advantage of viewing the parfait layers in their entirety before the dish is eaten.

PARFAITS OF SALMON AND TUNA TARTARE WITH OSETRA CAVIAR AND CRÈME FRAÎCHE

5 tablespoons olive oil

1 cup crème fraîche

2 large shallots, minced

2 tablespoons capers, drained and chopped

2 teaspoons grated lemon zest

4 teaspoons soy sauce

2 teaspoons grated fresh horseradish

2 tablespoons chopped fresh coriander

2 tablespoons chopped fresh chervil

10 ounces yellowfin tuna, diced

10 ounces salmon, ground

2 teaspoons coarse sea salt or kosher salt

2 teaspoons ground white pepper

10 ounces osetra caviar

8 slices thin white bread, toasted, crust removed, and cut into 4 triangles

SERVES

10

Guy Legay

preparation

Combine the shallots, vinegar, and wine in a small saucepan
and place over medium heat. Cook to reduce the liquid
by half. Stir in the cream and bring to a boil over
medium-high heat. Reduce heat to medium and gradually
whisk in the pieces of butter. Continue whisking
until all the butter has melted and the sauce is smooth.
Season with salt and white pepper. Pour the sauce
through a fine-meshed sieve lined with cheesecloth
into another small saucepan. Use the bottom of a sturdy ladle
to force as much liquid through the strainer as possible.
Set the saucepan with the sauce aside.

....

Rinse the sea scallops and pat them dry with paper towels.
Sprinkle the scallops with salt and white pepper
on both sides. In a large sauté pan or skillet,
melt 2 tablespoons of the butter over high heat.
When the butter foams, add 6 scallops and sear them
on both sides. Transfer the scallops to a plate and set aside.
Immediately repeat the process, discarding the old butter
and adding another 2 tablespoons after the second batch.
Repeat with the remaining scallops.

....

Place the saucepan with the butter sauce over
medium-low heat. Stir with a wire whisk to rewarm.
Carefully add the caviar, and stir gently
with a wooden spoon to combine.

....

To serve, spread the caviar butter in the center
of each of 4 serving plates. Arrange 6 scallops
in a circular pattern on top of the caviar butter.
Decorate each scallop with a small amount of caviar
and a chervil sprig. Serve immediately.

*Editor's note: This is a magnificent appetizer, worthy of the most sophisticated dinner party.
It sets the tone as well as the standard for the rest of the meal.*

SEARED SEA SCALLOPS WITH CAVIAR BUTTER

2 large shallots, minced

¼ cup white wine vinegar

¼ cup dry white wine

1 tablespoon heavy cream

1 cup (2 sticks) unsalted butter,
cut into small pieces

Salt and ground white pepper to taste

24 (about 1½ pounds) sea scallops

4 tablespoons unsalted butter

2 ounces beluga caviar

Garnish

1 ounce beluga caviar

24 fresh chervil sprigs

SERVES

4

Bernard Constantin

preparation

Place one 10–inch round doily and 1 nasturtium on each of 4 salad plates.

················

Grease, salt, and pepper eight 3½×1⅝-inch ramekins. Break an egg into each
of the ramekins. Transfer the ramekins to a heatproof dish and fill the dish two thirds
the way up the sides of the ramekins with hot water. Place the dish over medium heat and
cook the eggs until the whites have cooked but the yolks remain runny, about 10 minutes.
Transfer the ramekins to a protected countertop.

················

In a large sauté pan or skillet, melt the butter over medium heat. Add the prawns
and mushrooms, and sauté for 30 seconds. Stir in the shallot, wine, and cream
until the mixture thickens slightly. Adjust the seasoning with salt and black pepper.

················

Cut the bread into eight 3½×1-inch strips. Spoon the prawn mixture over the egg
in each ramekin, dividing it evenly. Place 2 ramekins on each of the 4 prepared plates.
Place 2 bread strips alongside the ramekins and serve immediately.

MY GRANDFATHER, HENRI CONSTANTIN, BOUGHT THE LARIVOIRE RESTAURANT
IN 1904. AT THAT TIME, IT WAS ALREADY WELL KNOWN
BECAUSE MONSIEUR LARIVOIRE HAD OPENED THE RESTAURANT IN 1860.
IT WAS A FORMER BOURGEOIS HOUSE ON THE BANKS OF THE RHÔNE
AT THE ENTRANCE TO LYONS. THE RESTAURANT'S EXCELLENT LOCATION
ENABLES CLIENTS TO EAT OUTSIDE BY THE ONE-HUNDRED-YEAR-OLD TREES
IN ADDITION TO EATING INSIDE IN THE SALONS.

MY FATHER, JACKY, TOOK OVER THE RESTAURANT IN THE 1940S.
HE WAS VERY SUCCESSFUL, AND THE RESTAURANT BECAME THE MEETING PLACE
OF LYONS NOTABLES.

AFTER TRAVELING AROUND EUROPE, THE UNITED STATES, AND ASIA,
I LEARNED MANY SECRETS OF HOW TO BECOME A GREAT CHEF
AND DECIDED TO TAKE OVER THE LARIVOIRE RESTAURANT IN 1980.
I RENOVATED THE RESTAURANT AND CREATED
A MORE MODERN STYLE OF COOKING BASED ON IMAGINATION.

PERHAPS MY THREE-YEAR-OLD DAUGHTER, CAMILLE CONSTANTIN,
WILL BE THE FOURTH-GENERATION CHEF…
BUT IT'S TOO EARLY TO TELL.

EGGS EN COCOTTE WITH DUBLIN BAY PRAWNS AND MORELS

4 unsprayed nasturtiums
Salt and ground black pepper to taste
8 large eggs
1 tablespoon unsalted butter
1½ pounds Dublin Bay prawns or
other large shrimp, peeled, deveined,
and cut into ½-inch dice
5 ounces morel mushrooms,
stemmed and cut into ½-inch dice
1 large shallot, chopped
2 tablespoons Madeira wine
1⅓ cups heavy cream
2 pieces of white bread, crusts
removed, toasted golden brown

SERVES

4

TOMATO TARTS WITH SEAFOOD AND TOMATO COULIS

4 medium Japanese eggplants

2 tablespoons olive oil

Tomato Concassée

2 large tomatoes

2 tablespoons olive oil

2 tablespoons chopped shallots

2 garlic cloves, minced

1 bouquet garni: 1 fresh parsley sprig,

1 fresh thyme sprig, and 1 bay leaf,

tied together in cheesecloth

Salt and ground white pepper to taste

Pinch of sugar

2 tablespoons unsalted butter

4 ounces white button

mushrooms, diced

1 tablespoon dried bread

crumbs (if needed)

Salt and ground white pepper to taste

4 medium-sized red tomatoes

Salt and ground white pepper to taste

1 teaspoon minced garlic

¼ cup olive oil

One 8-ounce puff pastry sheet

1 large egg, lightly beaten

1 tablespoon minced fresh thyme

Tomato Coulis

2 large ripe tomatoes

2 tablespoons olive oil

½ teaspoon minced garlic

1 rounded tablespoon minced

shallot or onion

Salt, ground white pepper,

and sugar to taste

24 cooked small shrimp,

bay scallops, or mussels

1 tablespoon minced fresh chives

1 tablespoon minced fresh basil

SERVES

4

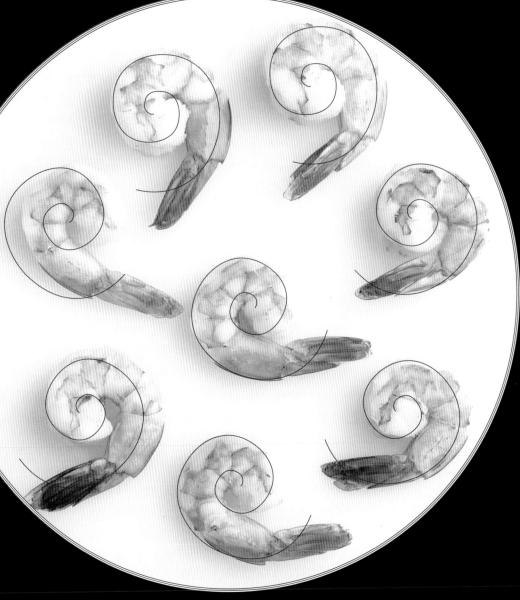

Roland Liccioni

RECIPE PHOTOGRAPH ON PAGE 16

preparation

Preheat the oven to 350 degrees F. Place the eggplants on a cutting board and slice in half lengthwise. Make slits in the flesh of the eggplants and, using a pastry brush, lightly brush the eggplants all over with the olive oil. Place the eggplants in a shallow pan and bake in the oven for 15 to 20 minutes, or until cooked through. Let cool to the touch. Separate the eggplant flesh from the skin and discard the skin. Dice the flesh, transfer to a plate, and set aside.

. . . .

To make the tomato concassée, blanch the tomatoes in rapidly boiling water for 20 seconds, drain, and submerge in a bowl of ice water. When the tomatoes have cooled, remove the skin and seeds, and dice.

. . . .

In a medium sauté pan or skillet, heat the oil over medium heat. Add the shallots and garlic, and sauté until the shallots are translucent, about 2 minutes. Add the diced tomatoes and bouquet garni, and simmer, uncovered, for 20 to 30 minutes, or until the water has evaporated. Season with salt, white pepper, and sugar. Stir the tomato concassée until well combined. Set aside.

. . . .

In a small sauté pan or skillet, melt the butter over medium-high heat. Add the mushrooms and sauté for 3 to 4 minutes. Remove from heat.

. . . .

In a medium bowl, combine the eggplant, mushrooms, and tomato concassée. If the consistency is too watery, add some of the bread crumbs, a little at a time, until the mixture is just moist. Season to taste with salt and white pepper.

. . . .

Blanch the 4 red tomatoes in rapidly boiling water for 20 seconds, drain, and submerge in a bowl of ice water. When the tomatoes have cooled, remove the skin and seeds. Cut the tomatoes into quarters and then lengthwise into ⅓-inch-wide strips. Season with salt and white pepper. In a small bowl, combine the garlic and olive oil. Add the tomato strips, stir carefully, and set aside.

. . . .

Preheat the oven to 375 degrees F. Lay out the puff pastry on a cool, dry work surface that has been sprinkled lightly with flour. Using a rolling pin, roll out the dough ⅛-inch thick. Carefully transfer the dough to a baking sheet and freeze for 10 minutes. Using a very sharp knife, cut four 1×13½-inch strips of dough. Set aside. Sprinkle the remaining dough with flour and roll it out again. Transfer this dough back to the baking sheet and freeze for 10 minutes. While the dough is still frozen, cut out four 4¼-inch-diameter circles. Prick each dough circle several times with a fork and place one in the bottom of each of 4 tart pans. Brush one side of the dough strips lightly with beaten egg and lay the strips, egg-side out, along the inside edge of the dough circles, pressing lightly to flatten as you go.

. . . .

Place the tart molds on a baking sheet and return to the freezer for 10 minutes. Remove the baking sheet from the freezer. Line each tart with parchment paper or aluminum foil and fill with pie weights or dried beans to prevent the dough from rising. Bake the tart shells in the oven for 10 minutes. Remove the baking sheet from the oven. Reduce the oven temperature to 350 degrees F.

. . . .

Divide the eggplant mixture among the 4 tarts and spread evenly with a rubber spatula or the back of a spoon. Arrange the marinated tomato strips on top of each tart in a decorative pattern. Sprinkle with thyme and bake the tarts in the oven for 10 to 15 minutes, or until the bottom of the tarts are lightly brown and cooked through. Remove them from the oven, let cool to the touch, unmold, and transfer the tarts to 4 salad plates.

. . . .

To make the tomato coulis, blanch the tomatoes in rapidly boiling water for 20 seconds, drain, and submerge in a bowl of ice water. When the tomatoes have cooled, remove the skins and seeds, and quarter. Heat the olive oil in a medium sauté pan or skillet over medium heat. Add the garlic and shallot or onion, and sauté until the shallot is translucent, about 2 minutes. Add the tomatoes and cook for 25 minutes. Pour the tomato mixture through a fine-meshed sieve into a small bowl. Use the bottom of a sturdy ladle to force as much liquid through the sieve as possible. Season with salt, white pepper, and sugar to taste. Allow the coulis to cool slightly.

. . . .

To serve, arrange the shrimp, scallops, or mussels on top of each tart and pour the tomato coulis around the tart. Garnish with chives and basil. Serve immediately.

Editor's note: The combination of tomatoes, eggplant, and seafood makes these tarts a versatile dish when planning any menu. They are also excellent for Sunday brunch.

Mario Buatta

preparation

Preheat the oven to 325 degrees F. Grease a 9×12-inch baking pan.

· · · · · · · · · · · · · ·

In a large bowl, combine the green chilies and cheeses. Spoon the mixture into the baking pan.

· · · · · · · · · · · · · ·

In a small bowl, combine the egg yolks, evaporated milk, flour, salt, and black pepper. Whisk until well blended.

· · · · · · · · · · · · · ·

In a large bowl, using an electric mixer set at medium-high speed, beat the egg whites until soft peaks form. Fold the egg whites into the yolk mixture. Pour the egg mixture over the cheeses. Using a fork, gently lift the cheeses to let the egg mixture seep through.

· · · · · · · · · · · · · ·

Bake in the oven for 30 minutes, or until the top is firm to the touch. Arrange the tomatoes in a decorative overlapping pattern around the edge of the casserole. Bake 30 minutes longer or until a toothpick inserted in the center of the casserole comes out clean. Cut into 3×4-inch squares. Serve hot or cold.

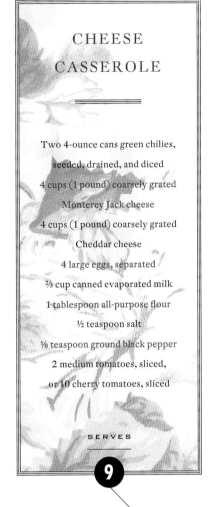

CHEESE CASSEROLE

Two 4-ounce cans green chilies, seeded, drained, and diced

4 cups (1 pound) coarsely grated Monterey Jack cheese

4 cups (1 pound) coarsely grated Cheddar cheese

4 large eggs, separated

⅔ cup canned evaporated milk

1 tablespoon all-purpose flour

½ teaspoon salt

⅛ teaspoon ground black pepper

2 medium tomatoes, sliced, or 10 cherry tomatoes, sliced

SERVES

9

The first time I was served this cheese casserole was at a 'cookout' in a New York City apartment. We were treated to steaks cooked over the wood-burning fire in the dining room fireplace, which were accompanied by slices and slices of cheese casserole and salad. It was the cheese casserole that won my heart as a great addition to our dinner. It can also be served as an appetizer or hors d'œuvre.

Joachim Splichal

preparation

In a medium sauté pan or skillet, melt ¼ cup of the butter over medium heat. Add the cèpe mushrooms and sauté briefly until the mushrooms begin to soften. Stir in one-third of the shallot and parsley, and sauté 1 minute more. Remove from heat and season with salt and white pepper. Using a slotted spoon, transfer the mushrooms to a plate and set aside. Discard the melted butter and the liquid remaining in the sauté pan. Repeat 2 more times, first with the chanterelles, then the shiitakes, adding one-third of the shallot and parsley mixture and ¼-cup butter, and cleaning the pan each time.

. . . .

Preheat the oven to 250 degrees F. Grease a 9×13-inch baking dish.

. . . .

To cook the fresh pasta, cut the pasta sheet into 2×3-inch rectangles and cook in salted boiling water until al dente. Drain in a colander. If using dried lasagna noodles, cook the pasta in salted boiling water according to package directions until al dente. Drain in a colander, then transfer the pasta to a cutting board. Using a very sharp knife, cut the noodles into 3-inch-long pieces and set aside.

. . . .

To assemble the individual lasagnas in the prepared baking dish, alternate 3 layers of pasta rectangles with each of the 3 mushroom mixtures, beginning with the pasta and ending with the mushrooms. Repeat to make 6 individual lasagnas.

. . . .

Bake in the oven, uncovered, for 20 minutes, or until warmed through.

. . . .

While the lasagnas are baking, place a small sauté pan or skillet over high heat and melt the 1 tablespoon butter. Add the celery hearts and sauté until crispy. Using a slotted spoon, transfer the celery hearts to a dish lined with paper towels and pat dry to remove the excess butter. Set aside.

. . . .

To make the truffle sabayon, melt 1 tablespoon of the butter in a medium sauté pan or skillet over medium heat. Add the shallots and sauté until translucent, about 2 minutes. Add the white wine and stir, then cook to reduce by half. Whisk in the truffle juice and the remaining 2 tablespoons plus ½ cup butter, and cook to reduce by one-fourth. Whisk in the heavy cream until well blended. Season with salt and white pepper.

. . . .

Using a metal spatula, transfer each lasagna to the center of each of 6 salad plates. Generously spoon some of the truffle sabayon over each lasagna and garnish each with a sprinkle of celery hearts. Serve immediately.

Editor's note: This dish is a delightful and delicious variation on traditional lasagnas — and will especially please mushroom-lovers. Serve it with a dry white wine and crusty bread.

LASAGNAS OF WILD MUSHROOMS WITH TRUFFLE SABAYON

Lasagnas
¾ cup unsalted butter
4 ounces cèpe (fresh porcini) mushrooms, thinly sliced
1 large shallot, minced
½ cup chopped fresh parsley
Salt and ground white pepper to taste
4 ounces black or white chanterelle mushrooms, thinly sliced
4 ounces shiitake mushrooms, stemmed and thinly sliced
½ pound fresh egg pasta in sheets, or 6 dried lasagna noodles

1 tablespoon unsalted butter
½ cup thinly sliced celery hearts
Truffle Sabayon
3 tablespoons plus ½ cup unsalted butter, cut into small pieces
2 tablespoons minced shallots
2 tablespoons dry white wine
¼ cup truffle juice (available in cans)
⅔ cup heavy cream
Salt and ground white pepper to taste

SERVES

6

With Clint Eastwood – Film Fest. 1990

This recipe is intimately linked to a genuine American memory.

Around 1987, my chefs and I spent two weeks at the Pierre Hotel in New York City attending a culinary event. A woman who was a famous food journalist from Pittsburgh, Pennsylvania, decided to celebrate her birthday during that time period. I felt both honored and scared. I had to be innovative, yet able to work with what was fresh and available in February. I knew she loved truffles and foie gras, so I invented this dish and served it to her the same evening. God was obviously with me, because the dish was very good, and still is today. Thank you, Mrs T. C., and thank you, New York City.

Christian Willer

preparation

Using a mandolin, V-slicer, or an extremely sharp knife, cut the potatoes crosswise into very thin, translucent slices.

• • • • • • • • • • • • • • •

Using a sharp knife, slice the truffles very thin. Form the truffle and potato slices into 'petals' by sandwiching 1 truffle slice between 2 potato slices, and place on a baking sheet. Repeat until all the truffle slices have been used.

• • • • • • • • • • • • • • •

In a medium sauté pan or skillet, melt 7 tablespoons of the butter over medium-high heat. Reduce the heat to medium, and using a metal spatula, gently add 4 potato petals. Fry them until they are golden and crisp on both sides. Carefully remove the petals from the pan and place them on paper towels. Gently pat the excess grease from the petals and immediately sprinkle with salt. Repeat until all the petals have been fried and salted.

• • • • • • • • • • • • • • •

Preheat the oven to 150 degrees F. Rinse the duck livers and pat them dry with paper towels. Season with salt and white pepper. In a medium sauté pan, melt 2 tablespoons of the butter over medium-high heat. Add the duck livers and sauté for 2 minutes on each side. Using a slotted spoon, transfer the duck livers to a plate and place them in the oven to keep warm. Discard the butter from the pan and return the pan to heat. Add the truffle juice and chicken stock to the pan and stir to scrape up the browned bits from the bottom of the pan. After deglazing the pan, increase the heat to high and cook to reduce the liquid by half. Whisk in the remaining 3 tablespoons butter. Continue whisking until the mixture is well blended.

• • • • • • • • • • • • • • •

To assemble, arrange 2 duck livers and an equal number of potato petals on each of 4 serving plates. Serve immediately, with the sauce on the side.

STEAKS OF FOIE GRAS WITH TRUFFLED PETALS OF POTATOES

═══════════

2 large Idaho potatoes, peeled

Two 1½-ounce fresh truffles, peeled (reserve peel for another use)

12 tablespoons (1½ sticks) unsalted butter, melted

Salt to taste

Eight 1½-ounce duck livers

Ground white pepper to taste

7 tablespoons truffle juice (available in cans)

3 tablespoons chicken stock

SERVES

4

SOUPS, STEWS, & CHILIS

Emeril Lagasse

RECIPE PHOTOGRAPH ON PAGE 36

preparation

PORTUGUESE KALE SOUP

2 tablespoons olive oil

1 pound chorizo or andouille sausage, cut into ½-inch-thick slices

1 large onion, chopped

6 to 8 garlic cloves, minced

¼ cup coarsely chopped fresh parsley

2 large potatoes, peeled and diced

4 quarts chicken stock

1 bunch kale, stemmed and torn

2 bay leaves

¼ teaspoon dried thyme

1½ teaspoons salt

¼ teaspoon red pepper flakes

Ground black pepper to taste

½ cup chopped fresh mint

SERVES

8

When I think of my childhood in Fall River, Massachusetts, I remember a happy blur of Portuguese festivals. They were wonderful celebrations of music, dance, and food from the old country. The feast was known as buon fester, or 'good festival', and the dish that stands out in my memory from the festival is suppische kaldene, or kale soup. This unusual soup was prepared many ways.

It often contained chorizo, split peas, and mint to accompany the base of kale, potatoes, and stock. When I became chef at Commander's Palace, I made kale soup for the staff, substituting the local andouille sausage for the Portuguese chorizo. The response was so enthusiastic that I began to run 'kale soup' as a special on the menu in the spring and fall when kale is in season in Louisiana. There is even a sweet little Portuguese song about suppische kaldene, but I'll spare you.

In a heavy 8- to 9-quart stockpot, heat the olive oil over high heat. Add the sausage and onion, and sauté for 2 minutes. Add the garlic, parsley, and potatoes, and cook for 2 minutes. Add the chicken stock and kale, and bring to a boil. Stir in the bay leaves, thyme, salt, pepper flakes, and black pepper. Reduce heat to medium and simmer, uncovered, until the potatoes are tender, about 30 minutes. Skim the fat from the top with a large spoon.

Pour the soup into individual soup bowls and stir ½ teaspoon of mint into each bowl. Allow the mint to steep and infuse its flavor for 1 to 2 minutes. Serve with crusty Portuguese or French bread.

Martha Stewart

preparation

In a small sauté pan or skillet, melt the butter over medium heat. Add the shallots and ground coriander, and sauté for 2 minutes. Set aside.

. . . .

In a large saucepan, combine the chicken stock, carrots, parsnips, and shallot mixture. Bring to a boil over high heat. Reduce heat to low, cover, and simmer for 35 minutes, or until the vegetables are tender. Place the mixture into a food processor fitted with a metal blade, or a blender. Pulse briefly to make a coarse purée.

. . . .

Return the mixture to the large saucepan and stir in the cream, salt, and white pepper. Cover and simmer over low heat for 5 minutes. Serve immediately in individual soup bowls, garnished with fresh coriander.

CARROT AND PARSNIP SOUP WITH CORIANDER

4 tablespoons unsalted butter
4 large shallots, minced
1½ teaspoons ground coriander
4 cups chicken stock
8 large carrots, peeled and sliced
2 large parsnips, peeled and sliced
½ cup heavy cream
Salt and ground white pepper to taste
1½ tablespoons chopped
fresh coriander (cilantro) leaves

SERVES

4

Editor's note: This is a great soup to serve all year round, because it lends itself to light summer dinners as well as hearty holiday celebrations.

CORN SOUP
WITH CLAMS
AND 'PETIT'
VEGETABLES

12 clams, scrubbed

⅓ cup salt

¼ cup cornmeal

Vegetables

1 small zucchini

3 quarts water

¼ cup coarse salt

⅓ cup ⅛-inch-diced carrots

⅓ cup ⅛-inch-diced turnips

⅓ cup ⅛-inch-diced celery

Lobster Cream

2 tablespoons olive oil

1½ medium unpeeled carrots, chopped

1½ stalks celery, finely chopped

¾ cup finely chopped leeks,

white and pale green part only

¾ cup finely chopped unpeeled turnips

1 small onion, finely chopped

3 tablespoons minced shallots

½ small bunch fresh parsley, stemmed

1 tablespoon coarse salt

1 teaspoon black peppercorns

3 pounds lobster shells from cooked

lobsters, heads included if possible

(ask your fishmonger for shells)

1 cup Chardonnay

5 cups heavy cream

3 quarts water

2 tablespoons coarse salt

Five 7-inch-long fresh ears

yellow corn, shucked, or 3 cups

frozen yellow corn kernels

Salt and ground white pepper to taste

½ cup dry white wine

1 tablespoon minced shallots

½ cup water

4 fresh dill sprigs

SERVES

4

I GREW UP
IN GASCONY
EATING SOUP.
MY FATHER,
WHO WAS ITALIAN
AND A VERY
HARD WORKER,

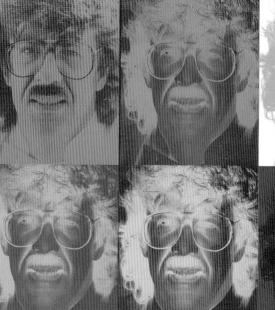

I ALWAYS HAD A POT
OF SOUP EVERY DAY
IN MY RESTAURANT.
I INCLUDE
HOT SOUPS
OR CONSOMMÉS
IN MY AUTUMN
AND WINTER MENUS.

THEY ARE ALWAYS
SERVED FROM
A TUREEN INTO
A GARNISHED
SOUP BOWL.
WHEN I ARRIVED
IN WASHINGTON,

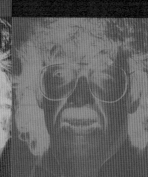

THERE WERE NO
INTERESTING SOUPS
ON THE MENUS,
SO I INTRODUCED
NEW VARIETIES SUCH
AS THIS
NOW-FAMOUS
CORN SOUP.

Jean-Louis Palladin

preparation

Place the clams in a large bowl and cover with cold water. Add the salt and cornmeal. Let the clams soak for at least 3 hours to expel any sand.

•••••••••••••

To prepare the vegetables, peel the outside flesh and skin from the zucchini in ⅛-inch-thick slices. Reserve the peeled zucchini for another use. Cut the zucchini peelings into ⅛-inch-dice. Set aside.

•••••••••••••

In a large saucepan, combine the water and salt. Bring to a boil over high heat. Add the carrots, turnips, and celery, and cook for 5 minutes. Add the zucchini peelings and continue cooking for 1 minute. Remove from heat. Pour the vegetables into a sieve and transfer them to a medium bowl containing ice water. Let the vegetables cool, then drain again. Transfer the vegetables to a medium bowl, cover, and refrigerate until ready to use. This may be done several hours before serving.

•••••••••••••

To make the lobster cream, heat a heavy 6-quart saucepan over high heat for about 1 minute. Add the olive oil, carrots, celery, leeks, turnips, onion, shallots, parsley, salt, peppercorns, and lobster shells. Cook for 5 minutes, stirring occasionally. Add the Chardonnay and bring to a boil. Reduce heat to low and simmer, uncovered, for 10 minutes, stirring occasionally. Add the cream, increase heat to high, and return to a boil. Reduce heat to low and simmer, uncovered, for 15 minutes more.

•••••••••••••

Remove the sauce from heat. Using a slotted spoon, remove and discard the larger shells. Pour the sauce through a fine-meshed sieve lined with cheesecloth into a medium bowl. Use the bottom of a sturdy ladle to force as much liquid through the sieve as possible. Use immediately or let cool slightly, cover, and refrigerate for up to 48 hours. Do not freeze.

•••••••••••••

If using fresh corn, combine the water and salt in a large saucepan. Bring to a boil over high heat. Add the corn and cook just until tender, about 3 minutes. Drain and cool in ice water. Drain again. Using a very sharp knife, cut the kernels from the cobs. If using frozen corn, cook the corn according to package directions. Place 2 tablespoons of the kernels in a small bowl, cover, and refrigerate until ready to use. Purée the remaining kernels in a food processor fitted with a steel blade, or a blender. Transfer the purée to a 4-quart saucepan and stir in 2½ cups of the lobster cream. Bring to a boil over high heat, stirring occasionally. Remove from heat. Pour the mixture through a fine-meshed sieve lined with cheesecloth into a medium saucepan. Use the bottom of a sturdy ladle to force as much liquid through the sieve as possible. Season with salt and white pepper. Set aside.

•••••••••••••

In a large sauté pan or skillet, heat the dry white wine over medium heat. Add the shallots, and cook for 5 minutes. Rinse the clams well and add them to the wine and shallots. Cover and steam for 5 to 10 minutes until the shells open. Remove from heat. Discard any clams that have not opened. Using a slotted spoon, transfer the clams to a plate and let cool. Remove the meat and reserve.

•••••••••••••

Place an ovenproof soup tureen in the oven and turn the heat to 350 degrees F.

•••••••••••••

To serve, in a small saucepan, reheat the clam meat in the ½-cup water over low heat for 4 to 5 minutes, being careful not to boil. Drain and set aside.

•••••••••••••

Spread a portion of the vegetable mixture, the reserved corn kernels, and the clam meat in the bottom of 4 shallow soup bowls. Pour the corn and lobster cream mixture into the hot tureen, garnish with dill sprigs and ladle the soup into the bowls at the table.

Bradley Ogden

preparation

*Editor's note: This flavorful dish is the 'lightest' version of a stew you will ever taste.
And, with all the fresh vegetables, it is also one of the healthiest. Reserve all of the trimmings
from the vegetables to add to the lobster broth.*

To make the court bouillon, in a stockpot large enough to hold all the lobsters, combine all
the bouillon ingredients except the lobsters. Cover and bring to a boil over high heat.
Reduce heat to low, add the lobsters head first, and simmer, uncovered, for 8 to 10 minutes,
or until a claw can be pulled off easily. Transfer the lobsters to a large bowl of ice water.
When cool enough to handle, drain, remove the meat from the shells, place on a plate,
and set aside. Reserve the shells for the broth.

. . . .

Fill a large pot outfitted with a basket for steaming two-thirds full of water. Cover and bring
to a boil over high heat. Arrange the fennel, turnip, corn, and beets in the basket.
Cover and steam for 4 minutes, or until the vegetables are tender.
Transfer the cooked vegetables to a large platter and set aside.

. . . .

Fill the basket with the asparagus, broccoli rabe, and peas. Cover and steam for 4 minutes
or until tender. Transfer the cooked vegetables to the platter. Fill the basket with the spinach
and tomatoes. Cover and steam for 3 minutes. Transfer the vegetables to the platter.

. . . .

To make the lobster broth, heat the olive oil over medium-high heat in a heavy
8- to 9-quart stockpot. Add the lobster shells and sauté, stirring occasionally.
Add the remaining broth ingredients and water to cover. Reduce heat to low and simmer,
uncovered, for 30 minutes. Using a slotted spoon, remove and discard the solid ingredients
from the broth. Pour the liquid through a fine-meshed sieve lined with cheesecloth
into a large saucepan. Set aside.

. . . .

To make the herb butter, place the butter and dill in a small bowl and mix with a wooden spoon.
Cover and refrigerate until ready to use.

. . . .

In a large pot of salted boiling water, cook the noodles according to package directions.
When the noodles are tender, remove from heat, drain, return them to the pot, and cover.

. . . .

Add the vegetables to the lobster broth and warm over low heat. Swirl in a little herb butter,
salt, and white pepper. Add the noodles and lobster meat. Serve in individual soup bowls.

LOBSTER AND VEGETABLE STEW WITH EGG NOODLES

Court Bouillon

5 quarts water

1¼ cups dry white wine

1 large onion, sliced

3 celery stalks, sliced

3 medium carrots, peeled and sliced

1 bouquet garni: 10 fresh parsley
sprigs, ¼ teaspoon red pepper flakes,
½ teaspoon black peppercorns, and
1 bay leaf tied together in cheesecloth

½ large lemon, seeded

Three 1½-pound live lobsters

½ cup julienned young fennel

½ cup peeled and diced turnip

½ cup corn kernels

½ cup peeled and diced small
golden beets

½ cup bias-cut asparagus pieces

½ cup broccoli rabe florets

½ cup green peas

½ cup baby spinach leaves

½ cup cherry tomatoes, stemmed

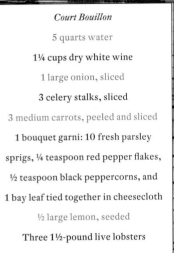

Lobster Broth

2 tablespoons olive oil

½ cup dry white wine

½ teaspoon saffron threads

2 large tomatoes, seeded and chopped

10 fresh chervil sprigs

½ teaspoon minced fresh tarragon

2 bay leaves

1 teaspoon minced lemongrass

Vegetable trimmings

Herb Butter

2 tablespoons unsalted butter, at
room temperature

1½ teaspoons minced fresh dill

12 ounces fresh egg noodles

Salt and ground white pepper to taste

SERVES

6

Shirley MacLaine

FAVORITE CHICKEN AND MUSHROOM SOUP

One 3-pound chicken, cut into pieces (reserve liver)

1 tablespoon vegetable oil

1 garlic clove, minced

1 teaspoon ground coriander

1 teaspoon ground black pepper

4 ounces white button mushrooms, stemmed and thinly sliced

1 chicken liver (from above), finely chopped

1 teaspoon soy sauce

SERVES 4

1 Rinse the chicken. Put the chicken pieces in a medium stockpot and add water to cover. Bring to a boil. Lower heat and simmer, uncovered, for 20 minutes. Remove the meat from the bones, reserving the bones, and cut the meat into small pieces. Reserve the broth in the stockpot.

2 Remove and discard the skin from the chicken. Transfer the chicken pieces to a plate and let cool. Set aside.

3 Put the bones back in the reserved broth in the stockpot and simmer, uncovered, over low heat for 2 hours. Drain the stock through a fine-meshed sieve into a medium bowl and set aside. In a medium pot, heat the oil over medium heat. Add the garlic and sauté for about 1 minute. Add the coriander, black pepper, mushrooms, chicken liver, and chicken meat. Cover and cook for 5 minutes, stirring occasionally. Add 4 cups of the reserved chicken stock and the soy sauce. Simmer, uncovered, 10 to 15 minutes longer. Serve hot.

Editor's note: This delicious soup has a delicate Asian flavor. For variety, add some shiitake mushrooms in place of the button mushrooms and garnish with chopped scallions.

James Garner

preparation

In a heavy 8- to 9-quart stockpot, brown half the ground beef over medium heat, breaking up any clumps that form as the meat cooks. Using a slotted spoon, transfer the meat to a bowl and set aside. Repeat with the remaining meat. Discard all but 2 tablespoons of grease in the stockpot.

. . . .

Sauté the onions in the grease over medium heat until they are translucent, about 2 minutes. Stir in the tomato sauce, cooked meat, chili powder, cumin, oregano, garlic powder, jalapeño, and the water. Simmer, uncovered, over low heat for 1 hour, stirring occasionally. If the mixture gets too thick, add more water. Skim off the grease. Season with salt and black pepper. Serve hot.

**THIS IS A RECIPE
THAT MY DAD
ALWAYS USED
TO MAKE**

W. W.
BUMGARNER'S
CHILI

6 pounds ground beef

2 large onions, finely chopped

Four 8-ounce cans tomato sauce

¼ cup plus 2½ tablespoons
chili powder

2½ tablespoons ground cumin

2½ tablespoons dried oregano

1½ tablespoons garlic powder

1 teaspoon minced jalapeño

2 cups water

Salt and ground black pepper to taste

SERVES

15

Jimmy Connors was playing Ivan Lendl in the semifinals of the U.S. Open. Just prior to the match, Jimmy had some of my chili. In the middle of the match, he ran off the stadium court for some bathroom relief.

Tony Trabert and Pat Summerall were the CBS Sports TV commentators and very graciously explained to the audience that the official rules allow for bathroom breaks during the match. Commentator John Newcombe added his own editorial: "Alan King's chili did him in."

Hello, my name isn't Billie Jean

Alan King

preparation

In a heavy 12-inch skillet, heat the olive oil over medium heat and sauté the onions, garlic, and red and green peppers. Stir over medium heat for 3 to 4 minutes until they are wilted but not browned. Add salt and black pepper to taste. Remove from heat. Place the vegetable mixture in a heavy 8- or 9-quart pot or Dutch oven.

. . . .

In the same 12-inch skillet, heat the vegetable oil over medium heat and brown half of the ground beef. Break up any clumps. Add salt and black pepper. Drain off any excess grease and add the browned meat to the pot with the vegetables. Repeat to cook the remaining ground beef.

. . . .

Once again using the 12-inch skillet, lightly brown the Italian sausage over medium-high heat and break up any clumps. Add the browned sausage to the pot.

. . . .

In the same skillet, lightly brown half the cubed steak over medium-high heat. Add more vegetable oil if needed. Repeat to cook the remaining steak. Remove the steak from the skillet and place in a bowl. Set aside.

. . . .

Place the pot with the vegetables and ground meat over medium heat and add the tomatoes along with their liquid. When the mixture begins to simmer, add the tomato paste, ground cumin, the 1 tablespoon black pepper, red pepper flakes, chili powder, lemon juice, oregano, thyme (rub the oregano and thyme between your palms before adding them to the pot), bay leaves, and pork bones. Stir until blended.

. . . .

If using dried red kidney beans, pick over and rinse them, and add them now. Add the 1 cup beef broth and bring the mixture to a boil. Cover the pot and reduce heat to low. Simmer for about 3 hours, or until the mixture begins to thicken and the meat becomes fairly soft. Add the steak and continue cooking for 2 more hours. Stir frequently during cooking and add more broth or water if the chili seems in danger of scorching. If using canned beans, drain and rinse them and add to the chili two hours after the steak. Continue to simmer 1 more hour whether you add canned beans or not.

. . . .

To serve, ladle the chili into individual bowls and top with red onions, scallions, vinegar, rice, and additional red pepper flakes. If storing in the refrigerator, let the chili cool to room temperature and then refrigerate for up to 5 days. To reheat, bring to a boil, reduce heat, and simmer until heated through, adding broth and adjusting the seasonings as needed.

U.S. OPEN CHILI

¼ cup olive oil

2 cups chopped onion

2 tablespoons minced garlic

¾ cup chopped red bell pepper

¾ cup chopped green bell pepper

Salt and ground black pepper to taste

½ cup light vegetable oil,
plus more as needed

5 pounds ground lean beef chuck

2 pounds hot Italian sausage,
removed from casings

4 pounds flank or skirt steak, cubed

Three 12-ounce cans Italian
plum tomatoes

One 12-ounce can Italian
plum tomato paste

1 tablespoon ground cumin

1 tablespoon ground black pepper

1 tablespoon red pepper flakes

2 tablespoons chili powder

2 teaspoons fresh lemon juice

3 tablespoons dried oregano

3 tablespoons dried thyme

4 bay leaves

1 or 2 small pork bones

1½ pounds dried red kidney beans,
or two 8¾-ounce canned dark red
kidney beans

1 cup beef broth or more as needed

Toppings

Chopped red onion

Chopped scallions, including
the green tops

Chili pepper vinegar

Steamed rice

Red pepper flakes

SERVES

20

Bob & Rod Jackson-Paris

COLORADO CHILI

One 28-ounce can plum tomatoes, drained and chopped

Two 8-ounce cans tomato sauce

1 large can diced green chilies (mild, medium, or hot to taste)

3 cups water

2½ pounds lean ham or lean pork cutlets

½ cup all-purpose flour

¼ cup vegetable oil

1 cup chopped onion

3 large garlic cloves, minced

1 teaspoon salt

1 teaspoon seasoned salt

Ground black pepper to taste

2 to 4 teaspoons minced jalapeño, according to taste

Fresh flour or corn tortillas, as accompaniments

SERVES

6–8

Rod's mom was coming to meet Bob for the first time, so there was tension in the air. We all agreed that good food can be a binding element in families, no matter what their structure. To cross an unknown bridge requires a full stomach, so Rod's mom decided to whip up a batch of her Colorado Chili. Rod cautioned that a gringo had entered the family, so two pots of chili were made: one mild, the other burning hot. The Colorado Chili and a lot of love did help build a bridge. From there, tradition grew. Now, whenever family members visit the Jackson-Paris home, two pots of Colorado chili warm their hearts and stomachs. Some people just need a bit more fire than others.

preparation

In a Dutch oven, combine the tomatoes, tomato sauce, green chilies, and the water. Cover and cook over low heat for 5 to 7 minutes.

....

Meanwhile, trim the excess fat from the meat and cut the meat into thin 2-inch-long strips. Place the flour and meat strips in a plastic bag and shake gently to coat. Remove the floured strips and set aside.

....

In a medium skillet, heat the oil over medium heat. Add the onion and garlic and sauté for 2 minutes. Add the meat strips and sauté until lightly browned. Drain off any excess oil. Add the meat, onion, and garlic to the ingredients in the Dutch oven. Stir in the salt, seasoned salt, and black pepper. Add the jalapeño. Bring the mixture to a rapid boil. Reduce heat to low, cover, and simmer 2 to 2½ hours. Stir occasionally with a wooden spoon.

....

Serve hot with fresh flour or corn tortillas.

Cynthia Rowley

preparation

In a Dutch oven, fry the bacon until crisp over medium-high heat. Transfer with tongs to paper towels and pat dry. Crumble the bacon into a small bowl and set aside. Pour off half the bacon drippings from the Dutch oven.

. . . .

Place the potatoes in a medium saucepan, add water to cover, and cook over medium-high heat for 7 to 10 minutes, or until tender. Drain, run the potatoes under cold water to stop them from cooking further, drain again, and set aside.

. . . .

Add the onion, bell pepper, garlic, and ground beef to the remaining bacon drippings in the Dutch oven and brown over medium-high heat. Add the tomatoes. Cover and simmer over low heat for 30 minutes. Add the potatoes and the remaining ingredients. Continue simmering over low heat, uncovered, for 15 minutes or until hot.

. . . .

Serve the stew on individual plates and garnish with bacon bits.

When I was little, my family went on camping trips. One of my fondest memories is when we gathered around the campfire and mom served us cowboy stew. The most essential thing about having cowboy stew was looking the part: fringed vest, boots, and, of course, a giant cowboy hat.

My brother and I would wait while my mother served us from a huge pot set over the campfire. Eating our meal from tin cowboy plates really made us feel like we were in the Wild West.

COWBOY STEW

6 bacon slices

7 small red new potatoes, peeled and diced

1 large onion, chopped

1 medium green bell pepper, seeded and chopped

1 garlic clove, minced

1½ pounds ground beef

Two 15-ounce cans stewed tomatoes

One 11½-ounce can corn kernels, drained

One 15½-ounce can kidney beans, drained

1 tablespoon chili powder

Salt and ground black pepper to taste

SERVES

8

The following recipe was passed on from my mother, Anne, to my wife, Beth. It originally had been a recipe for spaghetti sauce. While raising four children, my mother served spaghetti once a week. I tired of it, claiming it had too many carbohydrates, so my mother revised it, exchanging the Italian spices for chili powder and the spaghetti for kidney beans— and began serving chili.

Lou Holtz

preparation

In a heavy 12-inch skillet, heat the olive oil over medium heat. Add the garlic and sauté until lightly browned, about 2 minutes. Add the meat and brown. Break up any clumps that form as the meat cooks. Stir in the chili powder, vegetable juice cocktail, tomatoes, tomato sauce, and the water. Reduce heat to low and simmer, uncovered, for 1 hour. Stir in the kidney beans and continue simmering, uncovered, for 30 minutes.

. . . .

Serve in individual bowls. If desired, garnish with Cheddar cheese and chopped onion.

ANNE HOLTZ
CHILI

2 tablespoons olive oil
2 garlic cloves, minced
1½ pounds ground sirloin
3 tablespoons chili powder
One 46-ounce can vegetable
juice cocktail
One 16-ounce can whole
tomatoes, drained
One 15-ounce can tomato sauce
1½ cups water
One 15½-ounce can dark red kidney
beans, rinsed and drained
1 cup (4 ounces) grated
Cheddar cheese (optional)
1 medium onion,
finely chopped (optional)

SERVES

6

BREADS

This is a hearty snack that I generally enjoy 30 to 40 times per day when I'm supposed to be writing a column.

Dave Barry

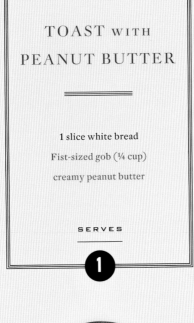

TOAST WITH
PEANUT BUTTER

1 slice white bread
Fist-sized gob (¼ cup)
creamy peanut butter

SERVES

1

preparation

You get yourself a slice of white bread—the kind with no fiber, vitamins,
or anything else healthy in it—and you put it in your toaster and push the lever down.
I like my toast well done, so I push the lever down 3 or 4 times, until the smoke detector
is beeping. Then I get a spoon and smear a fist-sized gob of peanut butter
(creamy, not chunky!) on the toast and eat it.

Hint: If you're in a hurry, you can skip the toast and put the peanut butter straight into your mouth.

· · · · · · · · · · · · · · · ·

Additional hint: If you're in a real hurry, you can also skip the spoon.

Sally Jessy Raphael

BAKED FRENCH TOAST

One 20-ounce loaf white bread,
cut into approximately ½-inch cubes

One 8-ounce package cream cheese,
cut into small cubes

12 large eggs

1½ cups milk

¾ cup maple syrup

SERVES

8

preparation

Note: The bread needs to soak overnight.

The night before serving, lightly coat
a 10×15-inch baking pan with vegetable oil
cooking spray or butter. Evenly distribute
half of the bread cubes in the dish.
Sprinkle the cream cheese on top
of the bread cubes. Evenly disperse
the remaining bread cubes on top.

· · · · · · · · · · · · · ·

In a large bowl combine the eggs, milk,
and syrup. Using an electric mixer
set at medium speed, beat the mixture
until it is well blended. Pour the mixture
evenly over the bread, making sure
every cube is moistened.
Cover and refrigerate overnight.

· · · · · · · · · · · · · ·

The next morning, preheat the oven to
350 degrees F. Bake the French toast
in the oven for 45 minutes, or until
golden brown. Serve immediately.

ONCE UPON A SLICE...

One day I was in my bed-and-
breakfast, the Issac Stover House,
and I was trying to come up with
something that everyone would like
for breakfast—something that would
make people feel like they were
eating at home. I created this
overstuffed French toast so that
guests never left hungry and had
plenty of energy to start their day.

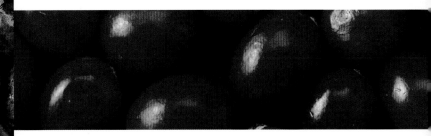

This recipe was once published in a major newspaper in my state of New Jersey. For the next few months, nearly every time I would meet a group of New Jerseyans, someone would say to me, "Senator Bradley, I saw your muffin recipe in the paper, and I made them the other day. Those are some of the best muffins I've ever had."

NEW JERSEY BLUEBERRY OR CRANBERRY MUFFINS

2 cups unbleached all-purpose flour

½ cup plus 1 tablespoon sugar

2½ teaspoons baking powder

¾ teaspoon salt

1 large egg, beaten

1 cup milk

⅓ cup vegetable oil

1 cup fresh or frozen blueberries
or cranberries

2 tablespoons confectioners'
sugar, sifted (optional)

MAKES

12

preparation

Preheat the oven to 400 degrees F. Grease a 12-cup muffin tin, or fill each cup of the tin with a paper liner.

. . . .

Sift the flour, the ½-cup sugar, baking powder, and salt together into a large bowl. Make a well in the center and set aside.

. . . .

In a small bowl, combine the egg, milk, and oil and whisk to blend. Pour the egg mixture into the well of the dry ingredients and mix with a wooden spoon just until blended. In a small bowl, combine the blueberries or cranberries with the remaining 1 tablespoon of sugar. Stir gently to coat all the berries. Carefully fold the blueberries or cranberries into the muffin batter.

. . . .

Fill the muffin cups about two-thirds full of batter. Bake for 25 minutes, or until a toothpick inserted into the center of a muffin comes out clean. Place the muffins on a wire rack to cool.

. . . .

Serve warm or cooled and, if desired, dusted with confectioners' sugar.

THE FIRST TIME I HAD THIS COFFEE CAKE, I WAS THIRTEEN YEARS OLD AND STAYING WITH A FAMILY IN CLEVELAND, OHIO. I WAS THERE FOR A JUNIOR COMPETITION BETWEEN THE UNITED STATES AND AUSTRALIA. I STAYED AT THE BOGGS'S HOUSE WITH ANOTHER MEMBER OF THE U.S. TEAM, PEANUT LOUIE. MRS. BOGGS BAKED THIS RECIPE FOR US WHEN WE ARRIVED, AND WE LOVED IT SO MUCH THAT WE HAD IT AS PART OF BREAKFAST, LUNCH, AND DINNER THAT WHOLE WEEK. WE WON THE TOURNAMENT, AND I'M SURE IT WAS DUE TO OUR HEALTHY TRAINING DIET! I HAVE BEEN MAKING THIS FOR FRIENDS AND FAMILY EVER SINCE, ESPECIALLY FOR CHRISTMAS BREAKFAST. HAPPY COOKING!

Tracy Austin

preparation

Preheat the oven to 350 degrees F. Grease and flour an 8-inch square cake pan.

. . . .

To make the streusel, combine the brown sugar, cinnamon, and pecans in a small bowl.
Stir the mixture with a fork and set aside.

. . . .

To make the batter, sift the flour, baking powder, baking soda, and salt together into a
medium bowl. In a large bowl, using an electric mixer set at the lowest speed,
cream the butter and sugar until light and fluffy. Add the eggs, one at a time, beating well
after each addition. Stir the dry ingredients into the egg mixture and blend thoroughly.
Combine the sour cream and vanilla, and fold into the egg mixture until smooth.

. . . .

Pour three fourths of the batter into the prepared cake pan. Sprinkle half of the streusel on top.
Add the remaining batter and cover the top with the rest of the streusel.

. . . .

Bake in the oven for 50 minutes, or until a toothpick inserted
in the center of the cake comes out clean.
Remove the cake from the oven and let cool in the pan
for 5 minutes before serving.

SOUR CREAM COFFEE CAKE

Streusel

½ cup packed brown sugar

2 teaspoons ground cinnamon

½ cup pecans, chopped

Cake Batter

2 cups unbleached all-purpose flour

1 teaspoon baking powder

1 teaspoon baking soda

½ teaspoon salt

1 cup (2 sticks) unsalted butter
at room temperature

1 cup granulated sugar

2 large eggs

1 cup sour cream

1 teaspoon vanilla extract

SERVES

12

Matzo Brie is one of our favorite dishes.

Although it is a traditional Passover dish,

it's one we enjoy all year-round.

When Steven isn't on location

shooting a new movie, he has

been known to whip up a batch or two

and share this delicious dish with

his staff at Amblin Entertainment.

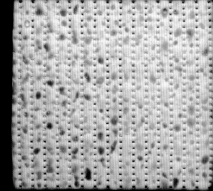

Steven Spielberg & Kate Capshaw

preparation

Break the matzos into large pieces and put them into a medium bowl. Add the cold water
and soak them for 1 minute, then drain.

. . . .

In a large bowl, lightly beat the eggs. Submerge the moist matzos in the eggs and let stand
for 5 minutes.

. . . .

In a large cast-iron skillet, melt the butter or margarine over medium heat.
Add the matzo and egg mixture. Cook, stirring occasionally, about 4 to 6 minutes,
or until the mixture becomes a light golden brown. Add salt and black pepper.
Transfer to a serving plate, and serve.

MATZO BRIE

4 whole matzos

2 cups cold water

6 large eggs

2 tablespoons unsalted butter
or margarine

Salt and ground black pepper to taste

SERVES

2–4

Hubert Keller

preparation

Place ¼ cup of the milk in a small bowl, add the yeast, and stir gently until the yeast is dissolved. Let stand for 5 minutes. Stir in the ¼ cup flour. Let stand for 10 minutes.

....

In the bowl of a heavy-duty mixer, combine the remaining flour, sugar, and a pinch of salt using a wooden spoon. Fit the mixer with a dough hook and set at medium speed. Add the eggs and remaining milk, and mix to blend. Add the ½ cup plus 2 tablespoons butter, a little at a time, and knead the dough for 5 to 8 minutes, until smooth. Add the raisins, kirsch, and yeast mixture and continue to knead the dough until it forms a soft ball. If the dough is sticky, add small amounts of flour. Transfer the dough to a lightly oiled large bowl, cover with a towel, and let the dough rise in a warm place for 1½ to 2 hours, or until it doubles in size. Punch the dough down.

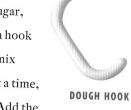

DOUGH HOOK

....

PASTRY BRUSH

Using a pastry brush, grease a 3-quart Kugelhopf mold or a bundt pan with the melted butter and place an almond in each runnel of the mold.

....

Press the dough into the mold. Cover the mold with a cloth and let the dough rise in a warm spot for 2 hours, or until it doubles in size.

....

KUGELHOPF MOLD

About 30 minutes before baking, preheat the oven to 400 degrees F. Bake the Kugelhopf in the oven for 45 minutes, or until it is golden brown and sounds hollow when tapped.
Unmold and transfer to a wire rack to cool.

....

When cool, dust the Kugelhopf with confectioners' sugar.
Cut into wedges to serve.

KUGELHOPF

===

1 cup milk at room temperature

1 cake compressed yeast
or 1 package active dry yeast

¼ cup plus 5 cups unbleached
all-purpose flour

¼ cup plus 2 tablespoons
granulated sugar

2 large eggs

½ cup (1 stick) plus 2 tablespoons
unsalted butter at room temperature

¼ cup raisins

2 tablespoons kirsch liqueur

1 tablespoon unsalted butter, melted

12 unskinned whole almonds

3 tablespoons confectioners'
sugar, sifted

SERVES

6–8

HUBERT KELLER

KUGELHOPF IS A RAISIN-AND-ALMOND BREAD
SERVED AT BREAKFAST OR WITH A GLASS OF
ALSATIAN WINE. IN THE OLD DAYS, THE DOUGH
WAS BEATEN BY HAND, BUT NOW OF COURSE,
I USE AN ELECTRIC MIXER.

Randy Travis

RECIPE PHOTOGRAPH ON PAGE 52

preparation

Preheat the oven to 375 degrees F. Using a heavy 12-inch iron skillet, lightly brown the hot Italian sausage over medium-high heat and break up any clumps. Using a slotted spoon, transfer the sausage to a large bowl (reserve ¼ cup for garnish) and discard the grease from the skillet. Put the vegetable oil or bacon drippings in the skillet. Place the skillet in the oven for 7 minutes, or until it is very hot.

....

In the meantime, add all the remaining ingredients to the sausage and stir just until blended.

....

Remove the skillet from the oven, and add the batter. Bake in the oven for 20 to 30 minutes, or until a toothpick inserted into the center of the bread comes out clean.

....

Sprinkle the top with the reserved sausage, cut the corn bread into wedges, and serve hot.

Editor's note: This corn bread is very spicy, very southern, and very festive. It's a great alternative to traditional corn bread.

MEXICAN CORN BREAD

1 pound hot Italian sausage, removed from casings

6 tablespoons vegetable oil or bacon drippings

One 7½-ounce box Martha White's Mexican corn bread mix or regular corn bread mix

2 cups self-rising cornmeal

3 large eggs, beaten

⅓ cup vegetable oil

1½ cups milk

One 16-ounce can creamed corn

½ cup chopped scallions, white and green parts

¼ cup chopped green bell pepper

1 tablespoon minced jalapeño

½ teaspoon red pepper flakes

2 tablespoons chopped pimiento

SERVES

6

You know, with this moustache, I really do look like Robert Goulet!

Roger Ebert

ABSOLUTELY FAT-FREE PANZAROTTI

Dough

1 cup warm (105 to
115 degrees F) water

1 package active dry yeast

2 cups whole-wheat flour

Filling

2 garlic cloves, minced

1 medium onion, minced

½ cup finely chopped
green bell pepper

4 ounces white button
mushrooms, sliced

1½ cups fresh spinach leaves

1 teaspoon dried basil

½ teaspoon dried oregano

½ teaspoon red pepper flakes

Salt and ground black pepper to taste

½ cup Pritikin fat-free marinara sauce
or other fat-free marinara sauce

1 cup (4 ounces) grated non-fat
mozzarella cheese

SERVES

2

MY WIFE AND I HAVE MADE TWO VISITS TO THE PRITIKIN LONGEVITY CENTER IN SANTA MONICA, CALIFORNIA. MY ORIGINAL PURPOSE WAS TO LOSE WEIGHT, BUT WHILE WE WERE THERE, I LEARNED A GREAT DEAL ABOUT HEALTH AND NUTRITION, AND IN PARTICULAR THE CONNECTION AMONG LONGEVITY, DAILY EXERCISE, AND A LOW-FAT, PRIMARILY VEGETARIAN DIET. PRITIKIN HAS A COOKING SCHOOL TAUGHT BY A TALENTED CHEF NAMED SUSAN MASSERON, WHO TRAINED IN BRITAIN AND ITALY. SHE INSPIRED US TO START COOKING THE LOW-FAT WAY, AND THIS RECIPE WAS ONE OF MY INVENTIONS. CHEERS.

preparation

Put the water in a small bowl, add the yeast, and stir gently until the yeast is dissolved. Let stand for 5 minutes.

....

Put the flour in a medium bowl and add the yeast mixture. Work the ingredients together using your hands to make a soft dough. If the dough is sticky, add a little more flour. Transfer the dough to a lightly floured work surface and knead until smooth, about 3 to 5 minutes. Put the dough in a bowl that has been lightly sprayed with vegetable-oil cooking spray. Cover with a towel and let the dough rise for 30 minutes, or until doubled in size. Preheat the oven to 425 degrees F. Spray a baking sheet with vegetable-oil cooking spray.

....

Return the dough to a lightly floured work surface and knead for 3 minutes. Divide the dough into 2 equal parts. Using a rolling pin, roll out the first half into a circle about 9 to 10 inches in diameter and about ⅛- to ¼-inch thick. Repeat the process with the remaining dough.

....

To make the filling, spray a large nonstick sauté pan or skillet with vegetable-oil cooking spray and place over medium heat. Add the garlic, onion, and green pepper, and sauté for 3 minutes. Add the mushrooms, spinach, basil, oregano, and red pepper flakes. Season with salt and black pepper. Stir and continue cooking for 3 more minutes. Remove from heat. Using a slotted spoon, transfer the vegetables to a medium bowl, add the marinara sauce and mozzarella, and gently stir to combine.

....

Spoon the vegetable mixture on one half of a dough circle. Fold the other half over, firmly crimping the edges, and poke the top 3 to 4 times with a fork to allow steam to escape. Repeat the process with the other dough circle.

....

Bake in the oven for 15 to 17 minutes, or until the panzarotti are crisp and golden. Remove the panzarotti from the oven and serve immediately.

COMPELLING STUFF, ★★★★, Dick Clark's latest piece — 'Corn Fritters' — is his most daring work so far. UNASHAMED THUMBS-UP!

preparation

In a medium bowl, combine the creamed corn, eggs or Eggbeaters, corn kernels, sugar or sugar substitute, salt, and white pepper. Mix well. Gradually stir in the flour and continue stirring until smooth.

· · · · · · · · · · · · · ·

Spray a large nonstick skillet with cooking spray or melt the butter over medium heat.

· · · · · · · · · · · · · ·

For each fritter, pour ¼-cup of batter into the preheated skillet and cook until golden brown on both sides. Stack them on a platter and serve with melted butter.

CORN FRITTERS

One 17-ounce can creamed corn

4 large eggs, or one 8-ounce package Eggbeaters, lightly beaten

1 cup frozen corn kernels, thawed

2 tablespoons sugar, or 2 packets sugar substitute

Salt and ground white pepper to taste

6 tablespoons all-purpose flour

Vegetable-oil cooking spray or 1 tablespoon unsalted butter

Melted unsalted butter for topping

MAKES

13

One of the big treats in my family was corn fritters. My mother usually served them on Sunday mornings. As a kid, I asked her why she called them fritters, and she explained to me that they were really corn 'oysters,' but if she called them 'oysters,' I wouldn't eat them! Fritters are really little balls of corn and batter that are deep-fried in fat. I'm sure I'd love them either way, but these corn fritters (oysters), made like pancakes, bring back fond memories of Sundays at home.

That was the new single 'Panzarotti' by Roger and the Eberts. It's got good texture, got my jaw moving, and has a taste that I'll remember for weeks. I give it a 100!

By the way Roger, I love what you're wearing… Did you lose your top two buttons too?

Tim Daly

CHEESE BOY

1 large flour tortilla

3 or 4 slices Cheddar cheese

2 or 3 slices roast turkey breast

½ cup alfalfa sprouts

SERVES

1

preparation

Place the tortilla on a microwavable plate. Lay the cheese slices on top of the tortilla and microwave on high for 30 seconds, or until the cheese has melted. Remove the tortilla from the microwave oven and place the turkey and alfalfa sprouts on the melted cheese. Fold in the sides of the tortilla and roll it like a burrito. Place it on a plate and serve immediately.

I was in SanteFe, New Mexico, playing the gentleman caller in The Glass Menagerie, when I had my first encounter with what now seems a ubiquitous presence in modern life: the microwave oven. The first thing I did was to put an egg in it to see if it would come out hard-boiled — it blew up. After several more experiments, all of them equally explosive, I finally stumbled on this delicious yet semi-healthy delicacy.

Alec Baldwin

VEGETARIAN
ENCHILADAS

═══════════

Sauce

2 tablespoons olive oil

1 medium onion, finely chopped

1 garlic clove, minced

Pinch of cayenne pepper

½ teaspoon hot sauce

1½ teaspoons chili powder

1 teaspoon honey

½ teaspoon salt

2 large tomatoes, peeled,
seeded, and chopped

One 8-ounce can tomato sauce

Filling

2 teaspoons olive oil

1 small onion, finely chopped

⅓ cup pitted black olives, sliced

1 garlic clove, minced

1 teaspoon chili powder

½ teaspoon salt

1¼ cups (10 ounces) mashed
pinto beans

8 corn tortillas

2 cups (8 ounces) grated
sharp Cheddar cheese

SERVES

4

preparation

Preheat the oven to 350 degrees F. To make the sauce, heat the olive oil in a large sauté pan or skillet over medium heat. Add the onion and garlic and sauté until the onion is translucent, about 2 minutes. Stir in the remaining sauce ingredients. Simmer, uncovered, over low heat for 30 minutes, stirring occasionally. Set aside.

To make the filling, heat the olive oil over medium heat in a medium sauté pan or skillet. Add the onion and sauté until translucent, about 2 minutes. Set aside 12 olive slices for garnish. Using a wooden spoon, stir in the remaining ingredients until well blended. If the mixture is very sticky, stir in some sauce.

To assemble, fill a tortilla with 3 to 4 tablespoons of filling and 1 tablespoon of the grated cheese. Roll the tortilla and place seam-side down in a shallow baking pan. Repeat to fill all the tortillas. Cover the tortillas with the sauce and sprinkle with the remaining cheese and the reserved olive slices.

Bake in the oven for 30 minutes, or until bubbling hot. Serve immediately.

Editor's note: This classic dish is delicious and easy to make. It's great for a casual dinner with friends and family, and a favorite of hungry teenagers. For a complete meal, serve with a salad and enjoy!

SALADS & VEGETABLES

Once, Danny Kaye told me that the only purpose of the scallop was to replace the fin of a shark in soups—you just need to poach scallops well and shred them. I thought about it and tried to discover something interesting about a poached scallop—finding it sweet, but without a pleasurable texture. I decided to concentrate the taste of the scallop and improve its consistency by cutting the flesh into thin slices and caramelizing them. The slightly tart orange butter brings out the sweetness of the scallop.

Roger Vergé

preparation

Trim each artichoke's stem to about ½ inch long. Wash the artichokes in salted water and drain, bottom up. Remove the thick, loose leaves around the base and cut off the tip of each remaining leaf with scissors. To a large saucepan half filled with water, add a pinch of salt, cover, and bring to a boil over high heat. Place the artichokes in the saucepan and cover. Return to a boil over high heat and cook for 25 to 35 minutes, or until a leaf is easily removed. Remove from heat, and drain the artichokes in a colander, bottom up, opening the leaves to release heat. Let cool.

. . . .

Remove most of the leaves from each artichoke, leaving only a few layers of the pale, tender inner leaves. Cut each artichoke in half lengthwise. Remove the fuzzy choke, leaving only the heart. Thinly slice the hearts into ⅛-inch-thick slices and set them aside.

. . . .

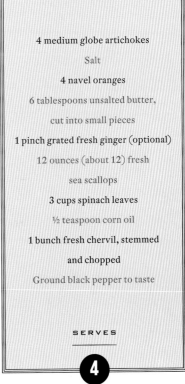

Cut off the peel and white pith from 2 of the oranges. Reserve 8 nice segments. Using your hands, squeeze the juice from the remaining orange segments. Using a juicer, squeeze the juice from the remaining 2 oranges. Place the juice in a small saucepan and cook it over medium heat to reduce to ¾ cup. Add a pinch of salt. Reduce heat to low. Whisking constantly, gradually add the butter. When the butter has melted completely, add the ginger, if desired. Transfer the mixture to a double boiler and keep warm over barely simmering water.

. . . .

Cut each scallop crosswise into 5 thin slices. Lay the slices of each scallop on a work surface, overlapping the 5 pieces to form a rose approximately 5 inches in diameter. Lightly sprinkle each scallop rose with salt.

. . . .

4 medium globe artichokes

Salt

4 navel oranges

6 tablespoons unsalted butter, cut into small pieces

1 pinch grated fresh ginger (optional)

12 ounces (about 12) fresh sea scallops

3 cups spinach leaves

½ teaspoon corn oil

1 bunch fresh chervil, stemmed and chopped

Ground black pepper to taste

Cover each of 4 salad plates with spinach leaves and distribute the sliced artichoke hearts over the spinach.

. . . .

Cut twelve 6-inch squares of parchment paper. In a medium sauté pan or skillet, heat the oil over high heat until it smokes. Place a parchment square over each scallop rose. Using a metal spatula, individually lift three roses and place them carefully in the frying pan with the parchment paper on top. Fry over very high heat for 4 to 5 minutes, or until the scallop roses caramelize.

. . . .

Gently transfer the scallops to the prepared salad plates, pull off the parchment paper, and set the scallops aside. Immediately repeat the process until all the scallops have been caramelized.

. . . .

SERVES

4

Drizzle each scallop rose with orange butter and decorate each plate with 2 of the orange segments and some chopped chervil. Sprinkle with black pepper and serve.

Peter Morton

preparation

Chill 4 salad plates. Arrange chicory, Belgian endive, and radicchio on the plates.

. . . .

In a medium sauté pan or skillet, heat the olive oil over medium heat. Add all the mushrooms. Sauté briefly until the mushrooms start to soften, about 2 minutes. Remove from heat and season with salt.

. . . .

Spoon the vinegar over the greens and top with the mushroom mixture. Garnish with the black pepper and chives. Serve immediately.

Editor's note: The mixture of wild mushrooms in this light yet flavorful salad makes it a perfect first course or luncheon entrée.

MUSHROOM SALAD WITH CHICORY, ENDIVE AND RADICCHIO

6 ounces chicory (curly endive), torn

6 ounces Belgian endive, torn

4½ ounces radicchio, torn

½ cup olive oil

½ ounce enoki mushrooms

1 ounce oyster mushrooms, thinly sliced

8 shiitake mushrooms, stemmed and thinly sliced

1 ounce silver dollar mushrooms, thinly sliced

Salt to taste

½ cup champagne vinegar

Ground black pepper to taste

4 tablespoons snipped fresh chives

SERVES

4

Vincent Guerithault

RECIPE PHOTOGRAPH ON PAGE 68

preparation

Cut the blue and yellow tortillas into strips. In a medium sauté pan or skillet, heat the olive oil over medium heat. Sauté the strips until crisp. Using a slotted spoon, transfer the strips to paper towels and gently pat them dry. Set aside. Remove the pan from the heat and reserve the warm olive oil.

· · · · · · · · · · · · · ·

Light a charcoal fire in a grill or preheat a gas grill to high.

· · · · · · · · · · · · · ·

In a large salad bowl, combine the bell peppers, ginger, basil, tomato, vinegar, 6 tablespoons of the reserved warm olive oil, salt, and black pepper. Whisk together until well blended. Add the tortilla strips and mixed greens. Gently toss. Divide equally among 4 individual serving plates.

· · · · · · · · · · · · · ·

Brush the shrimp with the remaining 2 tablespoons olive oil. Place the shrimp on the charcoal grill or reduce the temperature of the gas grill to medium and cook for approximately 1 to 2 minutes on each side, or until pink. Place the shrimp on top of the mixed greens and tortillas. Serve immediately

---

GRILLED SHRIMP SALAD WITH FRIZZLED TORTILLAS

Two 6-inch blue corn tortillas

Two 6-inch yellow corn tortillas

½ cup olive oil

2 tablespoons diced green bell pepper

2 tablespoons diced red bell pepper

2 tablespoons diced yellow bell pepper

1 tablespoon julienned fresh ginger

2 tablespoons chopped fresh basil

2 tablespoons diced tomato

2 tablespoons sherry wine vinegar

Salt and ground black pepper to taste

8 cups mixed greens

16 large fresh shrimp, peeled and deveined

SERVES

4

When I visit my parents in France, we eat a lot of salads and fresh fish from the Mediterranean. I like this recipe because it reminds me of summers in France, yet it incorporates a little of the Southwest, where I live now.

Lord Archer

OF WESTON-SUPER-MARE

preparation

Place the lettuce in a large salad bowl. Set aside. In a medium sauté pan or skillet, fry the bacon over medium heat until crisp. Transfer with tongs to paper towels and pat dry. Crumble the bacon into a small bowl and set aside.

....

Put the eggs in a medium saucepan, cover with cold water, and bring to a boil over high heat. Reduce heat to low and simmer 5 minutes for quail eggs or 12 minutes for hen eggs. Remove the pan from the heat and run cold water over the eggs until they are cool to the touch. Shell the eggs. Cut the quail eggs lengthwise into quarters or the hen eggs lengthwise into sixths. Set aside.

....

Peel, pit, and chop the avocado, and place in a small bowl. Add the lemon juice, and gently stir to blend. Add the bacon, eggs, avocado, and all the remaining salad ingredients to the lettuce and toss to mix.

....

To make the dressing, whisk the yogurt, mayonnaise, blue cheese, and salt and black pepper together in a small bowl until they are well blended.

....

Drizzle the desired amount of dressing on the salad, and toss gently. Serve immediately on salad plates.

I enjoy eating this salad when I am on my six-week writing spell in August and September. It is very light, so it doesn't make me feel sluggish during afternoon writing sessions.

SMOKED CHICKEN SALAD

Salad

1 bunch leaf lettuce, torn

4 ounces streaky bacon (traditional English bacon) or regular bacon

6 quail eggs, or 3 large hen eggs

1 medium avocado

2 tablespoons fresh lemon juice

1 pound smoked chicken breast, cut into thin strips

3 ounces white button mushrooms, quartered

¾ cup chopped cucumber

⅓ cup chopped scallions, including green tops

1 cup bean sprouts

½ cup raisins

1½ cups seasoned croutons

Dressing

1 cup (8 ounces) plain low-fat yogurt

2 tablespoons mayonnaise

½ cup (2 ounces) crumbled blue cheese

Salt and ground black pepper to taste

SERVES

4

Billie Jean King

preparation

Cook the rice according to package directions. In a wok or large sauté pan or skillet, heat the oil over medium-high heat. If using broccoli, cauliflower, or carrots, add them to the wok and sauté for 2 minutes. Add the rest of the vegetables and sauté for 2 minutes. Stir in the soy sauce and cook 1 minute longer.

· · · · · · · · · · · · · · · · ·

Transfer the rice to a large serving bowl. Using a slotted spoon, transfer the vegetables to another large serving bowl. Pour the liquid from the wok into a gravy boat to accompany the stir-fry. Serve immediately.

STIR-FRIED
VEGGIES

1½ cups uncooked rice
2 tablespoons extra virgin olive oil
2 pounds fresh vegetables, finely
chopped, such as broccoli, carrots,
cauliflower, mushrooms, pea pods,
onions, zucchini, and bamboo shoots
4 tablespoons soy sauce

SERVES

4

This vegetable and rice stir-fry represents good health to me. Since I went to the Maharishi Ayru-Veda Health Center in the spring of 1993 and became a vegetarian, I have found satisfaction in cooking up such delicacies as this one. Enjoy!

Hello, my name is
Billie Jean

Ceci n'est pas un Warhol...

PASTAS & SAUCES

Giorgio Armani

Tortelli alla Piacentina reminds me of my childhood, and I think everyone likes
to recall those memories. I am crazy about this dish and also very jealous.
You see, I love the extraordinarily delicate flavor of tortelli, and my jealousy
stems from my memories of the gestures and rituals of their preparation
that my mother always insisted on doing alone. As a matter of fact,
she still supervises their preparation whenever we cook together.

preparation

To make the filling, place the spinach in a large bowl.

Add the remaining filling ingredients and stir to combine. Cover and refrigerate.

. . . .

To make the pasta dough, place the flour on a work surface and make a well in the center.

Pour the 6 beaten eggs into the well.

Using a fork, slowly pull the flour from the inner edge into the egg.

Keep adding flour, a little at a time, until a soft dough is formed.

Begin kneading the dough. If it is sticky, continue adding flour in small amounts.

If it is dry, add the tepid water a little at a time.

Knead for 10 to 15 minutes, or until the dough is smooth.

Cover and set aside at room temperature for 30 minutes.

. . . .

Remove one-eighth of the dough and rewrap the remaining dough in a damp cloth

to prevent it from drying out.

Roll out the piece of dough with a rolling pin.

If using a hand-cranked pasta machine, set the rollers to their widest setting.

Feed the dough between the rollers while turning the crank.

Fold the dough in half and repeat until the dough feels smooth.

Gradually move the rollers closer together after each roll until the desired thickness is reached.

The pasta should be 5 inches wide, 1/16-inch thick, and as long as possible.

Cut the pasta into 5×4-inch diamonds.

. . . .

Place 1 level teaspoon of filling in the center of each diamond.

Using a pastry brush, moisten around the filling to the outside edges with the beaten egg.

Fold each diamond in half to make a triangle and crimp the edges firmly together to seal.

Transfer the tortelli one by one to a lightly floured towel, making sure they do not touch.

Repeat the process until all the dough has been used.

. . . .

Fill a large pot three-fourths full of water and bring to a boil over high heat.

With a large slotted spoon, carefully lower one-fourth of the tortelli into the boiling water.

As the tortelli surface, gently push them down with the slotted spoon until they have cooked

for approximately 5 minutes. Drain in a colander. Repeat until all the tortelli are cooked.

. . . .

In a large sauté pan, melt one-fourth of the butter over medium heat.

Add one-fourth of the tortelli and one-fourth of the grated Parmesan cheese.

Hold the pan by the handle and swirl it in a circular motion to ensure that the tortelli

are coated evenly with the butter and cheese.

Transfer to a large serving platter and cover to keep warm.

Repeat with the remaining 3 batches of tortelli.

. . . .

Sprinkle with black pepper and serve immediately.

TORTELLI ALLA PIACENTINA

Filling

1 pound spinach, washed, stemmed
and finely chopped

32 ounces ricotta cheese

2 large eggs, lightly beaten

1¾ cups (7 ounces) finely grated
Parmesan cheese

Salt and ground white pepper to taste

Pasta Dough

8½ cups semolina flour

6 large eggs, lightly beaten

⅜ cup tepid water, if needed

1 large egg, lightly beaten

Sauce

¾ cup (1½ sticks) unsalted butter

3 cups (12 ounces) finely grated
Parmesan cheese

Ground black pepper to taste

SERVES

10

Lidia Bastianich

preparation

To make the filling, heat the oil over medium heat in a large sauté pan. Add the leek and scallion and sauté until translucent, about 2 minutes. Add the Swiss chard or spinach, salt, and black pepper, and sauté for 1 minute. Remove from heat and stir in the parsley, egg, ricotta, salted ricotta, and Parmigiano. Mix well and set aside.

. . . .

To make the pasta dough, place the flour on a work surface and make a well in the center. Pour the 6 beaten eggs, oil, and salt into the well. Using a fork, slowly pull the flour from the inner edge into the egg. Keep adding flour, a little at a time, until a soft dough is formed. Begin kneading the dough. If it is sticky, add more flour in small amounts. If it is dry, add tepid water, a little at a time. Knead for 10 to 15 minutes or until smooth. Divide the dough into 2 equal pieces. Wrap one in a damp cloth to prevent it from drying out. Roll out the other piece with a rolling pin. If using a hand-cranked pasta machine, set the rollers to their widest setting. Feed the dough between the rollers while turning the crank. Fold the dough in half and repeat until the dough feels smooth. Gradually move the rollers closer together after each roll until the desired thickness is reached. The pasta should be 6 inches wide, the thickness of a linen napkin, and as long as possible. In the center of the first pasta sheet, place 1 tablespoon of filling at 2½-inch intervals. Using a pastry brush, moisten the pasta around the filling with the beaten egg. Place the second pasta sheet over the top of the filling, lightly pressing around each mound of filling. Using a ribbed 2½×3-inch cookie cutter, cut around each mound to create raviolacci. Transfer the raviolacci one by one to a lightly floured towel, making sure they do not touch. Repeat until all the pasta has been used.

. . . .

Fill a large pot three-fourths full of water and bring to a boil over high heat. With a large slotted spoon, carefully lower 10 or 12 raviolacci into the boiling water. Cook for 2 minutes, or until the raviolacci rise to the surface. Using a slotted spoon, remove them from the pot and drain in a colander. Repeat until all the raviolacci are cooked.

. . . .

To make the sauce, melt the butter over medium heat in a large saucepan. Stir in the milk, cream, and sage. Bring to a gentle boil for 3 minutes.

. . . .

Divide the raviolacci between 2 large sauté pans or skillets. Pour equal amounts of the sauce in each pan, turn heat to medium, and stir gently. Add half the Parmigiano to each pan and season with black pepper. Hold each pan by the handle and swirl in a circular motion until the sauce is reduced to a syrupy consistency and all the pasta has been coated with the sauce, about 2 minutes. Transfer to a large serving platter and serve immediately.

Editor's note: Homemade pasta may take some time to make, but after you taste this delicious stuffed Italian pillow of pasta, you'll agree it was worth it!

RAVIOLACCI
ALLE ERBE

Filling
1 tablespoon olive oil
¼ cup finely chopped leek, white part only
1 tablespoon minced scallion , white part only
½ cup minced Swiss chard or spinach leaves
1 teaspoon salt
1 teaspoon ground black pepper
¼ cup chopped fresh Italian parsley
1 large egg, lightly beaten
1 pound ricotta cheese
8 ounces salted ricotta, coarsely grated
½ cup (2 ounces) grated Parmigiano Reggiano

Pasta Dough
4 cups semolina flour
6 medium eggs, beaten
½ teaspoon olive oil
½ teaspoon salt
Tepid water, if needed
1 large egg, lightly beaten

Sauce
1 cup (2 sticks) unsalted butter
½ cup milk
½ cup heavy cream
16 fresh sage leaves, cut into thirds lengthwise
½ cup (2 ounces) grated Parmigiano Reggiano
Ground black pepper to taste

SERVES

8

Wolfgang Puck

THREE-CHEESE RAVIOLI

Filling

4 ounces fresh white goat cheese

2 ounces blue cheese

½ cup (2 ounces) grated
Parmesan cheese

Flesh of 1 small baked potato, mashed

2 large eggs

2 tablespoons chopped fresh chervil

2 tablespoons snipped fresh chives

Salt and ground white pepper to taste

Pasta Dough

1½ cups semolina flour

1½ cups unbleached all-purpose flour

2 teaspoons salt

4 large eggs

2 to 3 tablespoons olive oil

1 large egg, lightly beaten

Olive oil

Sauce

1 cup chicken stock

Ground white pepper to taste

½ cup (1 stick) unsalted butter
at room temperature, cut into
tablespoon-sized pieces

3 tablespoons grated
Parmesan cheese

1 tablespoon chopped fresh chervil,
plus 4 fresh chervil sprigs

1 teaspoon chopped fresh sage

1 teaspoon chopped fresh marjoram

Salt and ground white pepper to taste

SERVES

4

preparation

To make the filling, combine the goat cheese, blue cheese, Parmesan cheese, mashed potato, and eggs in a small bowl. Stir to mix well. Stir in the chervil and chives. Season with salt and white pepper. Cover and refrigerate until needed.

. . . .

To make the pasta dough, combine the flours, salt, 4 eggs, and 2 tablespoons of olive oil in a food processor fitted with a steel blade. Process until the dough holds together when pinched (add more olive oil if the dough appears dry). Transfer the dough to a lightly floured work surface and knead for 10 to 15 minutes or until smooth. Or, to make the dough by hand, place the flours on a work surface and make a well in the center. Pour the salt, 4 eggs, and 2 tablespoons of olive oil into the well. Using a fork, slowly pull the flour from the inner edge into the egg. Keep adding flour, a little at a time, until a soft dough is formed. Begin kneading the dough. If it is sticky, add more flour in small amounts. If it is dry, add more olive oil. Knead for 10 to 15 minutes until smooth. Wrap the dough tightly in plastic wrap and set aside at room temperature for 30 minutes.

. . . .

Remove half of the dough and rewrap the remaining dough in the plastic wrap to prevent it from drying out. Lightly dust a work surface with flour. Roll out the dough with a rolling pin. If using a hand-cranked pasta machine, set the rollers to their widest setting. Feed the dough between the rollers while turning the crank. Fold the dough in half and repeat until the dough feels smooth. Gradually move the rollers closer together after each roll until the desired thickness is reached. The pasta should be 5 inches wide, the thickness of a linen napkin, and about 30 inches long.

. . . .

To assemble the ravioli, dust a baking sheet with semolina. Brush the bottom half of a pasta sheet with the beaten egg. In the center of this section, place 1 heaping teaspoon of filling every 2 inches. Cover this section with the unbrushed half of the pasta and press the pasta around each mound of filling. Using a 2-inch cookie cutter, cut around each mound to create ravioli. Arrange the ravioli on the prepared baking sheet. Cover the baking sheet with plastic wrap and refrigerate until needed. Repeat to use the second half of the pasta.

. . . .

Fill a large pot three-fourths full with water, add a few drops of olive oil, and bring to a boil over high heat.

. . . .

Meanwhile, to make the sauce, pour the chicken stock into a medium saucepan and bring to a boil over medium-high heat. Season with white pepper. Whisk the butter, one piece at a time, into the stock. Cook until the mixture is slightly thickened, about 3 to 4 minutes. Stir in the Parmesan cheese. Reduce heat to low and cover to keep warm.

. . . .

Add the ravioli to the boiling water and cook for 5 minutes. Carefully remove the ravioli from the pot with a slotted spoon and drain on a clean towel.

. . . .

Add the chopped chervil, sage, and marjoram to the sauce and stir. Season with salt and white pepper. Add the ravioli and heat for 1 to 2 minutes.

. . . .

Divide the ravioli among 4 heated individual serving bowls. Spoon the sauce over the top and garnish each bowl with a small sprig of chervil. Serve immediately.

My mother used to make her own farmer cheese for cheese ravioli. Then she would add baked potato, chervil, black pepper, and salt to form rather large dumpling-style ravioli. Using goat, blue, and Parmesan cheeses gives the filling a more intense flavor.

Tricia Guild

preparation

In a large sauté pan or skillet, cook the pancetta over medium heat until it is slightly browned. Using a slotted spoon, transfer the pancetta to a plate and set aside.

· · · · · · · · · · · · · · · · · · · ·

In the same pan, heat 1½ tablespoons of the oil over medium heat. Add the onion and sauté until translucent, about 2 minutes. Add the celery and chili and sauté for 2 to 3 minutes. Return the pancetta to the pan and cook, uncovered, for 5 minutes while gradually stirring in the remaining 1½ tablespoons oil. Stir in the fennel seeds, wine, salt, and black pepper. Simmer, covered, over low heat for 10 to 15 minutes, stirring occasionally.

· · · · · · · · · · · · · · · · · · · ·

Fill a large pot three-fourths full with water and bring to a boil over high heat. Cook the pasta according to the package directions until al dente. Drain the pasta in a colander and return it to the pot. Add the sauce and Parmesan cheese, and mix well to coat the pasta. Transfer the pasta to a large serving platter and garnish with the celery leaves and chervil. Serve immediately.

CELERY AND PANCETTA WITH TAGLIATELLE

4 thin pancetta slices, chopped
3 tablespoons olive oil
1 medium onion, finely chopped
1 celery stalk, finely sliced
1 medium-sized dried
red chili, minced
½ teaspoon fennel seeds
¾ cup dry white wine
Salt and ground black pepper to taste
1 pound dried tagliatelle pasta
2 tablespoons freshly grated
Parmesan cheese
Chopped celery leaves
Minced fresh chervil

SERVES

4

Our family has a great love of Italian food, so we are always collecting recipes. A dear friend told me of a delicious pasta he had eaten with celery and some kind of seed! As I had fresh celery growing in the orchard, I sat him down to several summer lunches of tagliatelle and various kinds of celery sauces. We all found that this particular variation was the most delicious, and so this recipe has strong associations for me with summer lunches on our shady Tuscan terrace.

Harrison Ford

preparation

In a large sauté pan or skillet, heat the olive oil over medium heat. Add the onion and garlic and sauté until the onion is translucent, about 2 minutes. Add the anchovies, olives, capers, herbes de Provence or fresh herbs, and red pepper flakes. Sauté for 3 minutes. Stir in the tomatoes, salt, and black pepper, and simmer, uncovered, over low heat for 40 minutes.

. . . .

Fill a large pot three-fourths full with water and bring to a boil over high heat. Cook the pasta according to package directions until al dente. Drain the pasta in a colander and return it to the pot. Add the sauce and mix well to coat the pasta. Transfer the pasta to a large serving bowl and garnish with parsley. Serve immediately.

Editor's note: This thick tomato sauce is full of flavor and very versatile. Serve it over any shape of pasta or use it as a base for your next lasagna.

PASTA PUTTANESCA

¼ cup olive oil

1 medium onion, finely chopped

4 garlic cloves, minced

4 anchovy fillets, chopped

½ cup pitted, sliced black
Niçoise olives

3 tablespoons capers, drained

1 teaspoon herbes de Provence
or mixture of minced fresh basil
and oregano

½ teaspoon red pepper flakes

Two 15-ounce cans crushed tomatoes

Salt and ground black pepper to taste

1 pound dried pasta

¼ cup minced fresh Italian parsley

SERVES

4

Baroness Thatcher

preparation

Preheat the oven to 250 degrees F. To make the pork tenderloin, in a small bowl
combine the Parmesan cheese, basil, garlic if desired, salt, and white pepper.
Using your hands, completely coat the pork slices with the mixture.

· · · · · · · · · · · · · ·

In a large sauté pan or skillet, melt 2 tablespoons of the butter over medium-high heat.
Add the pork and sauté for 5 to 7 minutes on each side, or until it is cooked through.
Transfer the pork to a 9×12-inch baking pan. Cover and set aside.

· · · · · · · · · · · · · ·

In the same sauté pan or skillet, melt the remaining 1 tablespoon butter over medium heat.
Add the mushrooms and sauté until softened, about 2 minutes. Using a slotted spoon,
distribute the mushrooms evenly over the top of the pork slices.

· · · · · · · · · · · · · ·

To make the sauce, place the same sauté pan or skillet over medium-high heat. Add ¼ cup of
the chicken broth and stir to scrape up the browned bits from the bottom of the pan.
After deglazing the pan, whisk in the butter until melted. Add the flour and whisk until smooth.
Continue to whisk while adding the remaining ¾ cup broth, the cream, and any juices
that have collected in the bottom of the baking pan holding the pork. Bring to a boil
over medium-high heat, whisking continuously. Reduce heat to low and simmer for 4 minutes.
Turn off heat. Add the salt, pepper, Parmesan cheese, and mustard. Whisk to blend.
Pour the sauce over the pork and mushrooms, and cover the baking dish with aluminum foil.
Place in the oven to keep warm.

· · · · · · · · · · · · · ·

Fill a large pot three-fourths full with water and bring to a boil over high heat.
Cook the pasta according to package directions until al dente. Drain the pasta in a colander
and transfer it to a serving platter. Sprinkle the basil, chives, and parsley on top of the pasta
and toss to combine.

· · · · · · · · · · · · · ·

Remove the baking dish from the oven. Using a large spoon, place the pork on top of the pasta.
Spoon the mushrooms and sauce over the pork and pasta, and serve immediately.

*Editor's note: The wonderful flavor of the Dijon cream sauce complements the Parmesan
and basil-coated pork. This recipe is also delicious with beef or chicken.*

PASTA WITH PORK AND BASIL

═══════

Pork Tenderloin

2 to 3 tablespoons grated
Parmesan cheese

3 tablespoons minced fresh basil

1 garlic clove, minced (optional)

Salt and ground white pepper to taste

Two pounds pork tenderloin,
cut into 8 crosswise slices

3 tablespoons unsalted butter

6 ounces (1½ cups) white
button mushrooms, sliced

Sauce

1 cup canned unsalted chicken broth

2 tablespoons unsalted butter

1½ tablespoons all-purpose flour

½ cup heavy cream

Salt and ground white pepper to taste

2 tablespoons grated
Parmesan cheese

1¼ teaspoons Dijon mustard

1 pound fusilli or other dried pasta

2 tablespoons minced fresh basil

2 tablespoons snipped fresh chives

1 tablespoon minced fresh parsley

SERVES

4

PICCHIO PACCHIO

2 tablespoons extra virgin olive oil

1 large onion, finely diced

2 garlic cloves, minced

4 large tomatoes, peeled, seeded, and diced

7 fresh basil leaves, chopped

Salt and ground black pepper to taste

1 pound dried angel hair pasta or other dried pasta

SERVES

4

preparation

In a large saucepan, heat the olive oil over medium heat. Add the onion and garlic and sauté until the onion is translucent, about 2 minutes. Stir in the tomatoes and basil. Simmer, uncovered, over low heat for 30 minutes, stirring occasionally. Season with salt and black pepper. Set aside, and cover to keep warm.

. . . .

Fill a large pot three-fourths full with water and bring to a boil over high heat. Cook the pasta according to package directions until al dente. Drain the pasta in a colander and return it to the pot. Add the sauce and mix well to coat the pasta. Transfer the pasta to a large serving bowl. Serve immediately.

Sonny* and Mary Bono

*THE HONORABLE UNITED STATES
REPRESENTATIVE SONNY BONO (R-CALIFORNIA)

We serve this dish often. It's very healthy, and the amount of oil can be reduced to very little if you're watching your fat intake. In the summer, we'll make it along with a garden salad and enjoy it outdoors with a large group of friends. Sonny's perfect meal is this pasta, along with a grilled steak and a glass of any good Italian red wine.

MARY BONO

PASTAS & SAUCES

I

Gregory Peck

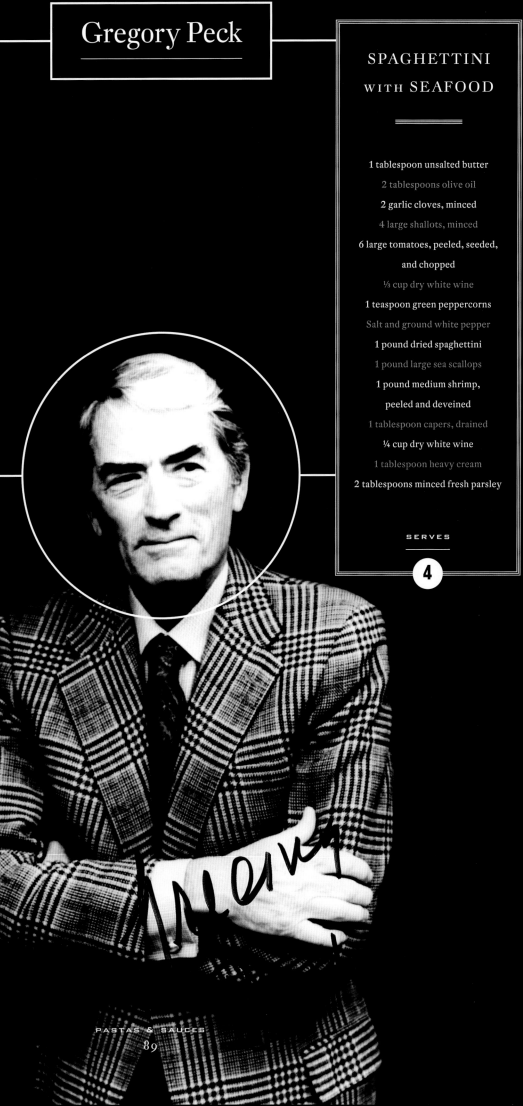

preparation

In a large saucepan, melt the butter with the olive oil over medium heat. Add the garlic and shallots, and sauté until the shallots are translucent, about 2 minutes. Stir in the tomatoes, the ⅓ cup white wine, green peppercorns, salt, and white pepper. Simmer, uncovered, over low heat for 20 minutes.

· · · · · · · · · · · ·

Meanwhile, fill a large pot three-fourths full with water and bring to a boil over high heat. Cook the pasta according to package directions until al dente. Drain the pasta in a colander, return it to the pot, and cover.

· · · · · · · · · · · ·

Add the scallops and shrimp to the sauce. Cook for 5 to 7 minutes or until the scallops are opaque and the shrimp are pink. Add the capers, the ¼ cup white wine, and cream to the sauce. Stir and bring to a boil. Immediately remove from heat.

· · · · · · · · · · · ·

Transfer the pasta to a serving platter. Spoon the sauce over the pasta. Sprinkle with parsley and serve immediately.

Editor's note: The combination of the seasonings, wine, and seafood makes this pasta sauce light and flavorful. It's a dish you'll want to serve time and time again.

SPAGHETTINI WITH SEAFOOD

1 tablespoon unsalted butter

2 tablespoons olive oil

2 garlic cloves, minced

4 large shallots, minced

6 large tomatoes, peeled, seeded, and chopped

⅓ cup dry white wine

1 teaspoon green peppercorns

Salt and ground white pepper

1 pound dried spaghettini

1 pound large sea scallops

1 pound medium shrimp, peeled and deveined

1 tablespoon capers, drained

¼ cup dry white wine

1 tablespoon heavy cream

2 tablespoons minced fresh parsley

SERVES

4

The ROMANS invented macaroni and shared it with the people of Lyons. Unlike the Italians, who love olive oil, the FRENCH prefer to use cream and butter with their PASTA...

Paul Bocuse

RECIPE PHOTOGRAPH ON PAGE 76

preparation

Preheat the oven to 400 degrees F.
Grease an oval gratin dish or a 10-inch
round casserole dish.

. . . .

Fill a large pot three-fourths full with water
and bring to a boil over high heat.
Cook the pasta according to package directions
until al dente. Drain the pasta in a colander,
return it to the pot, and cover.

. . . .

Melt the butter in a large saucepan over
medium heat. Gradually whisk in the flour
and mix well. Add the milk, salt, white pepper,
and nutmeg. Continuing to whisk,
bring the mixture to a boil. Let boil
for 1 minute. Stir in the cream and 1 cup
of the Beaufort or Gruyère cheese.
Slowly whisk until the cheese is melted.
Remove the saucepan from the heat.

. . . .

To assemble, arrange a layer of pasta on the
bottom of the prepared gratin or casserole dish.
Spoon one-third of the sauce over the pasta
and, if desired, sprinkle half of the truffle slices
on top. Repeat the process, ending with a layer
of the sauce. Sprinkle the remaining ½ cup
Beaufort or Gruyère on top and finish
with the Parmesan cheese.

. . . .

Bake in the oven for 20 minutes,
or until lightly browned.
Serve immediately.

MACARONI AND CHEESE

1 pound long macaroni,
or other dried pasta

7 tablespoons unsalted butter

6 tablespoons all-purpose flour

2 cups milk

1 teaspoon salt

Pinch of ground white pepper

Pinch of ground nutmeg

½ cup heavy cream

1½ cups (6 ounces) grated Beaufort
or Gruyère cheese

1 truffle, cleaned and
thinly sliced (optional)

5 tablespoons grated
Parmesan cheese

SERVES

6

LUNCHTIME GLOOP

"My kids love this. I only make it when my wife, Tabby, isn't home.
She won't eat it, in fact doesn't even like to look at it."

   2 cans Franco American Spaghetti (without meatballs)
   1 pound cheap, greasy hamburger

Brown hamburg in large skillet. Add Franco American Spaghetti and cook
till heated through. Do not drain hamburg, or it won't be properly greasy.
Burn on pan if you want – that will only improve the flavor. Serve with
buttered Wonder Bread.

                              Stephen King

BRENDA SCHWARZKOPF'S SEAFOOD LASAGNA

8 lasagna noodles

2 tablespoons unsalted butter or margarine

1 large onion, finely chopped

One 8-ounce package cream cheese, cubed, at room temperature

1½ cups (12 ounces) cream-style cottage cheese

1 large egg, lightly beaten

2 teaspoons dried basil

½ teaspoon salt

⅛ teaspoon ground white pepper

Two 10¾-ounce cans cream of mushroom soup

⅓ cup milk

⅓ cup dry white wine

1 pound cooked large shrimp, peeled, deveined, and cut in half widthwise

Three 6-ounce cans crabmeat, drained, rinsed, flaked, and picked over

¼ cup (1 ounce) grated Parmesan cheese

½ cup (2 ounces) shredded sharp Cheddar cheese

SERVES

9

preparation

Preheat the oven to 350 degrees F. Grease a 9×12-inch baking dish. Fill a large pot three-fourths full with water and bring to a boil over high heat. Cook pasta according to package directions until al dente. Drain the pasta in a colander and rinse it with cold water. Drain again. Set aside.

·················

In a large sauté pan or skillet, melt the butter or margarine over medium-high heat. Add the onion and sauté until translucent, about 2 minutes. Add the cream cheese and stir until well blended. Add the cottage cheese, egg, basil, salt, and white pepper. Stir until smooth. Set aside.

···············

In a large bowl, combine the soup, milk, and wine. Stir to blend. Add the shrimp and crabmeat. Continue to stir until well incorporated.

···············

To assemble the lasagna, arrange 4 noodles in the bottom of the prepared baking dish. Using a large spoon, spread half of the cheese mixture on top of the noodles. On top of this, spread half of the soup mixture. Repeat the process. Top with the Parmesan cheese.

···············

Bake in the oven, uncovered, for 45 minutes, or until lightly browned on top.

···············

Remove the lasagna from the oven and sprinkle it with Cheddar cheese. Return to the oven for 2 to 3 minutes, or until the cheese has melted.

···············

Transfer the lasagna to a wire rack. Let cool for 15 minutes. Cut into 3×3-inch squares to serve.

The Schwarzkopf family has very diverse tastes when it comes to food. It seems we can never agree on the same thing. However, seafood lasagna is one meal that we all like. Needless to say, it is one of the more popular recipes in our household, and I am delighted to share it with you. Hope you enjoy it as much as we do.

Fill a large pot three-fourths full with water and bring to a boil over high heat. Cook the pasta according to package directions until al dente. Drain the pasta in a colander and return it to the pot. Add the sauce and mix well to coat the pasta. Transfer to a large serving bowl and garnish with the 5 whole basil leaves and the 1 tablespoon parsley. Serve immediately.

When we serve pasta, we usually make this sauce and pass around a hunk of Parmigiano Reggiano and a small grater and let people grate their own.

PASTA with SIMPLE TOMATO SAUCE

2 tablespoons extra virgin olive oil

8 to 10 garlic cloves, halved lengthwise

1 teaspoon red pepper flakes

Two 28-ounce cans crushed plum tomatoes

1 teaspoon sugar

Salt and ground black pepper to taste

10 large fresh basil leaves, cut in thirds lengthwise, plus 5 large whole fresh basil leaves

½ cup plus 1 tablespoon minced fresh Italian parsley

1½ pounds dried pasta

SERVES

6

Mike Myers

KD with Wieners

Cook the macaroni according to package directions (it's best when cooked al dente, or as my dad would say, "all denty"). Drain the macaroni in a colander and return it to the pot. Add the contents of the cheese sauce packet, the margarine, and milk. Stir over low heat until smooth.

Turn off the heat and cover.

Place the hot dogs in a small saucepan and cover with water. Bring to a boil over high heat and cook, uncovered, for 5 minutes. Transfer the hot dogs to a cutting board and cut into bite-sized pieces.

Add the hot dog pieces to the macaroni and cheese, and stir until well combined. Transfer the mixture to 4 individual serving bowls and serve immediately.

In Canada, Kraft macaroni and cheese is called Kraft dinner, or K.D. This is the dinner that my dad would cook for me and my brothers while my mom was at night school. We would watch "Hockey Night in Canada" and eat Kraft dinner with wieners. My dad was in the British army, and he always said that the two most important things he learned were proper foot care and the ability to cook for one hundred people. For me, Kraft dinner is pure comfort food.

Sally Sirkin Lewis

After my ex-husband's
successful bypass surgery nearly
twelve years ago, he entered the Pritikin
Longevity Center in hopes of changing his
lifestyle and eating habits. He was very flexible
and adapted well to the essentially tasteless food.
I, however, couldn't bear the strange pasta sauces
suggested for people who need to subsist on low-fat
diets. So I challenged myself to do my own version.
This sauce is the result. It is wonderful on penne,
spaghetti, and linguine, and in lasagna and other
pasta casseroles. I always prepare the sauce in large
quantities and freeze it in pint and quart-size
freezer bags. Frozen, the sauce will keep
wonderfully for 2 to 3 months.

ENJOY!

preparation

Lightly spray the bottom of a 10-quart stockpot with vegetable-oil cooking spray and heat
over medium heat. Add the garlic and lightly sauté. Add the turkey, pork, and veal.
Brown over medium-high heat, using a wooden spoon to break up any lumps that form
as the meat cooks. Drain off the excess liquid. Add the mushrooms, tomatoes, purée,
tomato sauce, and tomato paste. Stir until well blended. Add the salt, black pepper,
Italian seasoning, and ketchup. Continue to stir until the mixture is blended.
Reduce heat to low, cover, and simmer for 1½ hours, stirring occasionally.
Uncover and add the basil and parsley. Adjust the seasoning with salt and black pepper
and add sugar if desired. Cover the pot and simmer for 30 minutes.

Note: Bring the sauce to room temperature before storing in the refrigerator or freezer.

PASTA SAUCE

10 to 12 garlic cloves, sliced

1 pound turkey breast, ground

1 pound pork loin, ground

1 pound white milk-fed veal, ground

18 to 20 jumbo white mushrooms,
stemmed and chopped

Three 28-ounce cans peeled
Italian tomatoes, drained

Three 28-ounce cans tomato purée

Three 15-ounce cans tomato sauce

One 15-ounce can tomato paste

Salt and ground black pepper to taste

3 tablespoons Italian seasoning

3 tablespoons ketchup

¾ cup packed minced fresh
basil leaves

2½ cups packed stemmed and
minced fresh parsley

½ teaspoon sugar (optional)

SERVES

20–30

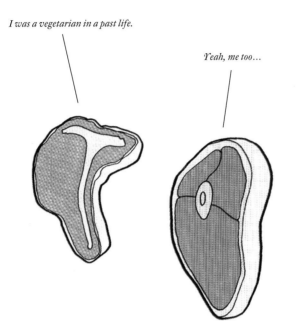

I was a vegetarian in a past life.

Yeah, me too...

MEATS

Short Ribs Miroton is an old family recipe

that was served in the Café Boulud in Lyons, France.

My grandmother Francine, who is in her nineties now,

used to prepare this dish, and still enjoys preparing it today.

It is an example of la cuisine à la récherche des goûts perdus:

THE CUISINE OF REDISCOVERING LOST FLAVORS.

Daniel Boulud

preparation

Cut the short ribs into pairs and trim the fat. In a large bowl, combine the short ribs, wine, onion, bacon, bouquet garni, salt, and black pepper. Mix well. Cover the bowl and refrigerate for 8 hours or overnight.

. . . .

Preheat the oven to 425 degrees F.

. . . .

Strain the marinade into a medium bowl and reserve the drained ingredients and the marinade. In a roasting pan on top of the stove, melt the butter over high heat. Add the short ribs and bacon. Sauté over high heat for 10 to 12 minutes. Add the reserved marinated onion and bouquet garni, stir well to combine, and cook for 10 minutes. Sprinkle with the flour and bake in the oven for 5 to 7 minutes.

. . . .

Place the roasting pan on the stove over medium heat. Using 2 large spoons, toss the ingredients well for 3 minutes. Add the reserved marinade and the potatoes. Season with salt and black pepper to taste. Mix well, cover with a tight-fitting lid, and bake in the oven for 50 to 60 minutes, or until tender. Mix well every 15 minutes to ensure even cooking.

. . . .

Discard the bouquet garni. Sprinkle the ribs with parsley and serve immediately in the roasting pan.

SHORT RIBS MIROTON

3 pounds beef short ribs, about 2 inches thick

1 bottle dry white wine

1 medium onion, quartered

4 bacon slices, cut into ½-inch pieces

1 bouquet garni: 2 fresh thyme sprigs, 6 fresh parsley stems, and 1 bay leaf tied together in cheesecloth

1 tablespoon salt, plus more to taste

1 tablespoon ground black pepper, plus more to taste

2 tablespoons unsalted butter

2 tablespoons all-purpose flour

2 pounds medium-sized red or white potatoes, halved

6 fresh parsley sprigs

SERVES

4

Jason Alexander

preparation

In a medium bowl, combine the salt, white pepper, paprika, and garlic powder.
Generously rub the brisket with the spice mixture (it should cling to the meat).
Place the brisket on a plate, cover it with plastic wrap, and refrigerate for at least 6 hours.

· · · · · · · · · · · · · ·

In a heavy pot or Dutch oven, combine the carrots, celery, green pepper, and onion.
Add the ¾ cup water. Bring to a boil over high heat. Reduce the heat to medium-low
and place the meat on top of the vegetables. Cover the pot and cook for 1 to 1½ hours
or until tender, turning every 20 minutes to ensure even cooking. Transfer the meat
to a cutting board and let stand for 5 minutes. Using a carving knife, slice the meat
against the grain, keeping the meat in its natural shape.

· · · · · · · · · · · · · ·

With a slotted spoon, transfer the vegetables to a food processor fitted with a metal blade
or a blender. Pulse briefly to purée. If the purée is too thick, add some of the cooking liquid.

· · · · · · · · · · · · · ·

Quarter the potatoes and add them to the liquid in the pan. Place the meat on top of the potatoes
and pour the vegetable purée over the meat and potatoes.

· · · · · · · · · · · · · ·

Return the pan to the stove and bring the liquid to boil over high heat. Reduce the heat to low
and simmer, covered, for 30 minutes or until the potatoes are tender.

· · · · · · · · · · · · · ·

Using 2 large spoons, carefully transfer the sliced meat to the center of a serving platter.
Surround the meat with the potatoes. Whisk together the liquid and vegetable purée remaining
in the pot. Pour the mixture into a gravy boat and serve alongside the pot roast and potatoes.

MOMMA G'S POT ROAST

¼ cup salt

¼ cup ground white pepper

¼ cup paprika

¼ cup garlic powder

2 pounds beef brisket

2 carrots, peeled and chopped

2 celery stalks, chopped

1 medium green bell pepper, seeded and chopped

1 medium onion, chopped

¾ cup water

8 red new potatoes

SERVES

4

My parents both worked throughout my childhood, so dinnertime was really quality time. We would sit and talk (mostly about my day), make jokes, and tell stories. The fact that we could drag dinner on for hours may have something to do with my ever-present 'battle of the bulge.' My mom is a great cook. She believes in large portions, and turns a cold shoulder on nouvelle cuisine. When she makes her pot roast, she also usually bakes a chicken, because "It's possible someone doesn't like pot roast." I have yet to meet that someone. This recipe is a big favorite. It's not exactly low fat, but if you watch the quantities, it ain't bad. It's from me and mom with love. Enjoy!

OSSO BUCO

Veal Stock

5 pounds veal bones

1 tablespoon unsalted butter

1 large carrot, peeled and diced

1 medium red onion, diced

2 celery stalks, diced

2 large tomatoes, quartered

2 teaspoons tomato paste

4 quarts water

1 bouquet garni: 1 fresh parsley sprig,
1 fresh thyme sprig, and 1 bay leaf
tied together in cheesecloth

20 black peppercorns

Tomato Concassée

2 large tomatoes

2 tablespoons olive oil

2 tablespoons minced shallots

2 garlic cloves, minced

1 bouquet garni: 1 fresh parsley sprig,
1 fresh thyme sprig, and 1 bay leaf
tied together in cheesecloth

Salt and ground white pepper to taste

Pinch of sugar

Osso Buco

½ cup all-purpose flour

8¼ pounds veal shanks,
cut into 2-inch-thick pieces

¼ cup olive oil

4 carrots, peeled and diced

1 large onion, diced

1 celery stalk, diced

¾ cup dry white wine

4 garlic cloves

1 bouquet garni: 1 fresh parsley sprig,
1 fresh thyme sprig, and 1 bay leaf
tied together in cheesecloth

1 medium lemon

1 medium orange

½ cup water

¾ cup sugar

1 pound dried pasta

2 tablespoons minced fresh parsley

SERVES

6

Bien que je suis un chef français et cette recette est d'origine Italienne, je prépare souvent l'osso buco en automne et en hiver quand famille et amis désirent un repas consistant et savoureux.

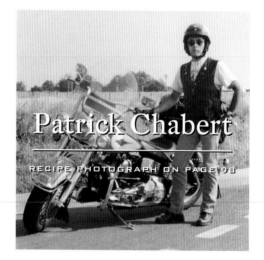

Patrick Chabert

RECIPE PHOTOGRAPH ON PAGE 98

Although I am a French chef and this recipe originated in Italy, I often cook osso buco in the fall and winter when family and friends want a hearty and flavorful meal.

preparation

To make the veal stock, preheat the oven to 350 degrees F. Rinse the veal bones and pat them dry with paper towels. Put the veal bones in a roasting pan large enough to hold them in a single layer. Bake in the oven until browned, approximately 40 minutes. Set aside.

. . . .

In a medium sauté pan or skillet, melt the butter over medium-high heat. Add the carrot, onion, and celery, and sauté until the onion is translucent, and the vegetables are tender, about 4 minutes. Stir in the tomatoes and tomato paste.

. . . .

In a 5-quart stockpot, combine the veal bones and vegetables. Add the water, bouquet garni, and black peppercorns, and bring to a boil. Reduce the heat to low and simmer, uncovered, for 3 hours. Skim any foam that comes to the top. Strain the stock through a fine-meshed sieve into a large bowl. Discard the solid ingredients. Return the stock to the pot and bring to a boil over high heat. Cook to reduce by half. Remove from heat and set aside.

. . . .

To make the tomato concassée, blanch the tomatoes in rapidly boiling water for 20 seconds, then submerge them in a bowl of ice water. When the tomatoes have cooled, remove the skin and seeds, and dice. In a medium sauté pan or skillet, heat the oil over medium heat. Add the shallots and garlic and sauté until the shallots are translucent, about 2 minutes. Add the tomatoes and bouquet garni, and simmer, uncovered, for 20 to 30 minutes, or until the water has evaporated. Add the salt, white pepper, and sugar. Set aside.

. . . .

To make the osso buco, preheat the oven to 450 degrees F. Place the flour in a shallow bowl. Dredge the veal pieces in the flour until completely coated. Shake off any excess flour. In a roasting pan large enough to cook the veal pieces in a single layer, heat the oil in the oven. Add the veal pieces and sear on all sides. Reduce the oven temperature to

350 degrees F, and transfer the veal pieces to a plate covered with paper towels. Add the carrots, onion, and celery to the roasting pan and cook over low heat for about 4 minutes. Increase the heat to medium-high, add the wine and stir to scrape up any browned bits from the bottom of the pan. After deglazing the pan, cook until all the liquid has evaporated. Return the meat to the pan and add enough veal stock to cover two-thirds of the veal. Add the garlic cloves and bouquet garni, and bring to a boil over high heat. Cover and bake in the oven for about 1½ hours, or until tender.

. . . .

Meanwhile, peel the lemon and orange. Cut the peels into thin julienne. In a small saucepan, blanch the lemon and orange julienne in boiling water and drain. Repeat 2 times. In another small saucepan, combine the ½ cup water and sugar. Heat over medium heat until the mixture is clear, then boil for 1 minute. Reduce heat to low, add the orange and lemon julienne, and cook for 2 to 3 minutes. Using a slotted spoon, transfer the orange and lemon julienne to a plate and set aside.

. . . .

Fill a large pot three-fourths full with water and bring to a boil over high heat. Cook the pasta according to package directions until al dente. Drain the pasta in a colander, return it to the pot, and cover.

. . . .

Transfer the veal to a serving platter and cover with aluminum foil to keep warm.

. . . .

Transfer the roasting pan to the stovetop, discard the bouquet garni, and cook over high heat to reduce the sauce by one-third. Add the orange and lemon julienne.

. . . .

To serve, divide the pasta among 6 large soup bowls. Arrange the osso buco on top of the pasta and spoon the sauce over it. Garnish each veal shank with the tomato concassée and parsley.

BAECKEOFFE OF PINK BEEF TENDERLOIN

1 medium red onion

3 pounds center-cut beef tenderloin

2 cups Alsatian Riesling

White Stock

1 to 1½ pounds veal or beef bones,
cut into 3- or 4-inch pieces
and blanched

6 cups cold water

1 large carrot, peeled and
coarsely chopped

1 medium onion, coarsely chopped

1 stalk celery, coarsely chopped

3 green leek leaves

2 unpeeled garlic cloves

3 whole cloves

1 bouquet garni: 1 fresh parsley sprig,
1 fresh thyme sprig, and 1 bay leaf
tied together in cheesecloth

1½ pounds medium Idaho potatoes

1 large turnip, peeled and
thickly sliced

2 carrots, peeled and thickly sliced

1 head Savoy cabbage, shredded

Sea salt and ground white pepper
to taste

⅓ cup grated horseradish

SERVES

6

Emile Jung

preparation

Note: The tenderloin needs to be marinated overnight.

In a dish just large enough to hold the meat, combine the red onion and the tenderloin.
Pour the wine over the meat and onion. Tightly cover the dish with plastic wrap
and refrigerate overnight, turning the meat occasionally.

. . . .

To make the white stock, place the bones, water, carrot, onion, celery, leek leaves, garlic,
cloves, and bouquet garni in a medium stockpot. Bring to a boil over medium heat,
then immediately reduce heat to low and simmer, uncovered, for 3 hours. Skim off any foam
that comes to the surface. Strain the stock through a fine-meshed sieve lined with
cheesecloth into a large bowl. If preparing ahead of time, set the bowl of stock in a bowl
of ice water to cool. When cool, refrigerate until needed.

. . . .

Remove the meat from the refrigerator and place on a plate. Strain the marinade
through a fine-meshed sieve into a small bowl and discard the onion. Reserve the marinade.

. . . .

Quarter the potatoes and place in a Dutch oven. Add the turnip, carrots, cabbage, white stock,
and wine marinade. Cover and cook over medium-low heat for 35 minutes. Add the meat,
salt, and white pepper. Cover and simmer for 30 minutes or until tender. Transfer the meat
to a cutting board and let it rest for 10 minutes before slicing.

. . . .

Using a slotted spoon, remove the vegetables and arrange around the outside edge
of a serving platter, alternating colors. Place the pot with the cooking liquid over high heat
and cook to reduce to 2 cups.

. . . .

Using a carving knife, slice the meat into 12 equal pieces. Place the meat in the center of the
serving platter. Spoon the reduced liquid around the beef and on top of the vegetables.
Serve with the horseradish.

This recipe is a local and traditional dish from Alsace done with a modern touch.
It was served to the Comité Colbert, an organization consisting of the heads
of prestigious French commercial enterprises such as Parfum Guerlain,
Chanel, and Lacoste. They are all connoisseurs and greatly enjoyed this dish.

Thomas Britt

I associate this recipe with my home in the Hamptons, and the oh-so-many great parties under the Moroccan tent with good friends.

preparation

Preheat the oven to 350 degrees F. Rinse the lamb and pat it dry with paper towels. Transfer the lamb to a roasting pan. Rub the oil vigorously over the lamb, then coat it with the garlic, rosemary, salt, and white pepper.

....

Roast the lamb in the oven, uncovered, for 1½ to 2 hours or until the juices run clear. Transfer the lamb to a cutting board, reserving the drippings in the pan, and let stand 5 minutes before slicing. Slice the lamb and arrange the pieces on a serving platter. Cover with aluminum foil and set aside.

....

To make the gravy, skim the fat before placing the roasting pan over medium-high heat. Add ½ cup of the water and stir, scraping up the browned bits from the bottom of the pan. After deglazing the pan, in a small bowl combine the flour with the remaining ¼ cup water and stir to mix. Pour the flour mixture into the pan and, while whisking continuously, add the butter. Bring the gravy to a boil and cook to the desired thickness. Whisk in the heavy cream until well blended. Pour the gravy into a gravy boat.

....

Place the mint jelly in a small serving dish and serve with the lamb and gravy.

BONELESS ROLLED LEG OF LAMB WITH GRAVY

3 pounds boneless rolled leg of lamb

⅓ cup olive oil

3 to 4 garlic cloves, minced

1½ tablespoons minced fresh rosemary

Salt and ground white pepper to taste

Gravy

¾ cup water

1½ tablespoons all-purpose flour

4 tablespoons unsalted butter

½ cup heavy cream

One 10½-ounce jar mint jelly

SERVES

6

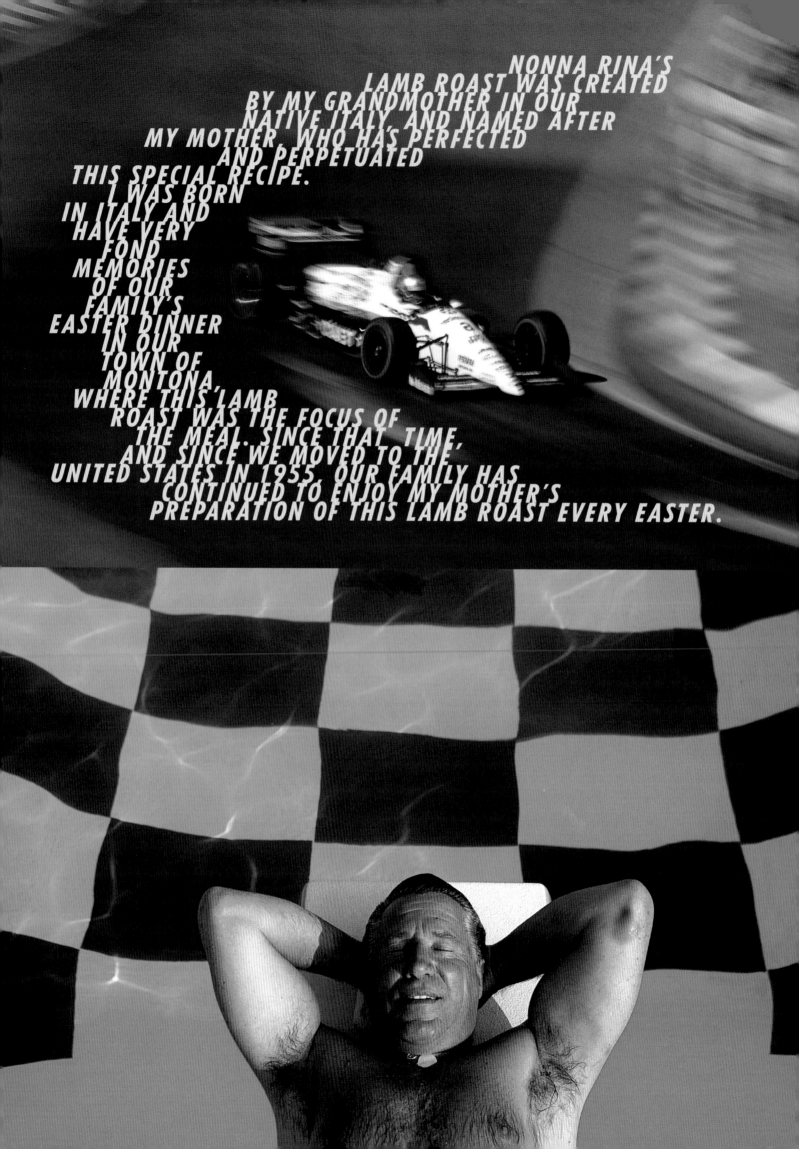

NONNA RINA'S LAMB ROAST WAS CREATED BY MY GRANDMOTHER IN OUR NATIVE ITALY, AND NAMED AFTER MY MOTHER, WHO HAS PERFECTED AND PERPETUATED THIS SPECIAL RECIPE. I WAS BORN IN ITALY AND HAVE VERY FOND MEMORIES OF OUR FAMILY'S EASTER DINNER IN OUR TOWN OF MONTONA, WHERE THIS LAMB ROAST WAS THE FOCUS OF THE MEAL. SINCE THAT TIME, AND SINCE WE MOVED TO THE UNITED STATES IN 1955, OUR FAMILY HAS CONTINUED TO ENJOY MY MOTHER'S PREPARATION OF THIS LAMB ROAST EVERY EASTER.

Mario Andretti

preparation

Preheat the oven to 350 degrees F. Rinse the lamb briefly and pat it dry with paper towels. Transfer the lamb to a large plate. Rub the lemon vigorously over the lamb, then coat with rosemary, Accent, salt, and black pepper. Set aside.

. . . .

In a small bowl, combine the Washington's Golden seasoning with the water to make a broth. Stir until dissolved.

. . . .

Place the celery, carrot, and onion into a roasting pan large enough to hold the leg of lamb. Pour the broth over the vegetables and place the lamb on top. Roast the lamb in the oven, uncovered, for 3 hours, or until the meat falls away from the bone. Baste every 20 minutes. Transfer the lamb to a cutting board, reserving the drippings, and let stand for 5 minutes. Slice the lamb and arrange the pieces on a serving platter. Cover with aluminum foil and set aside.

. . . .

To make the gravy, skim off the fat before pouring the reserved drippings through a sieve into a medium saucepan. Dissolve the cornstarch in the water and stir to combine. Pour the cornstarch mixture into the reserved drippings and, while whisking continuously, bring to a boil over medium-high heat. Cook to the desired thickness. Pour the gravy over the meat and serve.

NONNA RINA'S LAMB ROAST

One 7-pound leg of lamb, trimmed of fat

1 large lemon, halved and seeded

4 tablespoons minced fresh rosemary

Accent seasoning to taste

Salt and ground black pepper to taste

2 envelopes (each .13 ounce) G. Washington's Golden seasoning, or other concentrated seasoning mix or bouillon

2 cups warm water

2 celery stalks, chopped

1 carrot, peeled and chopped

1 medium onion, chopped

Gravy

Reserved drippings from cooked lamb, above

1 tablespoon cornstarch

½ cup cold water

SERVES

6–8

Alain Pic

LAMB LOIN WITH GARLIC CREAM, LOVAGE, AND CRISPY RAVIOLI

1½ tablespoons sesame oil

8 ounces cubed leg of lamb

Salt and ground white pepper to taste

Lamb Stock

1 tablespoon olive oil

1 tablespoon unsalted butter

5 pounds lamb bones plus scraps

2 garlic cloves, peeled

3 fresh thyme sprigs

1 bay leaf

½ cup dry white wine

2 cups chicken stock

Garlic Cream

5 heads garlic, divided into cloves

⅓ cup plus 1 tablespoon heavy cream

plus more if needed

1 tablespoon cold unsalted butter

Salt and ground white pepper to taste

Lamb Ravioli

3 teaspoons olive oil

Marinated lamb meat, above

1 tablespoon minced shallots

1 tablespoon soy sauce

2 tablespoons lamb stock, above

1 tablespoon minced fresh parsley

Salt and ground white pepper to taste

16 wonton sheets

1 large egg, lightly beaten

Two 1-pound lamb loins

Salt and ground white pepper to taste

3 tablespoons olive oil

Lamb stock, above

3 cups vegetable oil

2 tablespoons chopped fresh lovage

or celery leaves

SERVES

4

preparation

In a shallow bowl, combine the sesame oil and cubed lamb meat. Stir to coat, and season with salt and white pepper. Cover the bowl with plastic wrap, and refrigerate for 1 hour.

· · · · · · · · · · · · · ·

Meanwhile, to make the lamb stock, heat the olive oil and butter in an ovenproof casserole or Dutch oven over medium heat. Add the lamb bones and scraps. Brown over medium-high heat, stirring occasionally. Lower heat to medium and add the garlic, thyme, and bay leaf. Add the white wine and stir to scrape up the browned bits from the bottom of the pan. After deglazing the pan, reduce heat to low and add the chicken stock. Simmer, uncovered, for 25 minutes. Using a slotted spoon, remove and discard the solid ingredients from the stock. Pour the liquid through a fine-meshed sieve lined with cheesecloth into a medium bowl. Set aside.

· · · · · · · · · · · · · ·

To make the garlic cream, cut the garlic cloves in half. Fill a medium saucepan half full with water. Cover and bring to a boil over high heat. Add the garlic and cook for 2 minutes. Drain and transfer the garlic to a medium bowl containing ice water. Let cool and drain again. Repeat this process 2 times.

· · · · · · · · · · · · · ·

In a small saucepan, combine the garlic, cream, and butter. Place over high heat and bring to a boil. Reduce heat to low, cover, and simmer until the garlic is tender, about 10 to 15 minutes. Pour into a blender and purée until the mixture is smooth. If the mixture is too thick, add more cream. Return the garlic cream to the small saucepan, and season with salt and white pepper. Cover and set aside.

· · · · · · · · · · · · · ·

To make the ravioli, heat 1½ teaspoons of the olive oil in a medium nonstick sauté pan or skillet over high heat. Add the marinated lamb meat and brown on all sides, stirring constantly with a wooden spoon. Transfer the lamb to paper towels and pat dry. Place the lamb in a food processor fitted with a steel blade. Process for 10 seconds, or until the meat is ground.

· · · · · · · · · · · · · ·

Place the pan used to brown the lamb over high heat and add the remaining 1½ teaspoons of olive oil. When the oil is hot, add the ground lamb. Cook until crispy. Reduce heat to low, stir in the shallots, and cook for 1 minute. Increase the heat to medium-high, add the soy sauce, and stir to scrape up the browned bits from the bottom of the pan. After deglazing the pan, stir in the lamb stock, parsley, salt, and white pepper. Set aside.

· · · · · · · · · · · · · ·

To assemble the lamb ravioli, brush a wonton sheet with some of the beaten egg. Place 1 teaspoon of the lamb mixture in the center and place another wonton sheet on top. Press firmly around the edges to seal. Using a 2½-inch cookie cutter, cut around the filling. Repeat the procedure until all 8 ravioli are made. Set aside.

· · · · · · · · · · · · · ·

Preheat the oven to 450 degrees F. Season the lamb loins thoroughly with salt and white pepper. In an ovenproof sauté pan or skillet add the oil and sear the lamb over high heat on all sides. Bake in the oven for 6 minutes for rare and 8 minutes for medium rare. Transfer the lamb to a carving board. Pour off the fat from the pan. Place the pan over high heat, add the remaining lamb stock, and stir to scrape up the browned bits from the bottom of the pan. After deglazing the pan, cook to reduce the liquid to 1 cup. Set aside.

· · · · · · · · · · · · · ·

Rewarm the garlic cream over low heat, stirring occasionally. Set aside and keep warm.

· · · · · · · · · · · · · ·

In a large sauté pan or skillet, heat the vegetable oil over high heat to 375 degrees F, or until smoking. Using a slotted spoon, carefully place all the ravioli in the pan and fry until golden, about 45 seconds. Using a slotted spoon, transfer the ravioli to paper towels.

· · · · · · · · · · · · · ·

To serve, place 2 tablespoons of garlic cream in the center of each of 4 serving plates. Cut both lamb loins into 8 equal slices, and arrange 4 slices around the garlic cream on each plate. Place 2 ravioli at the top of each plate and spoon the reduced lamb stock around the bottom. Garnish each serving with 1½ teaspoons lovage or celery leaves. Serve immediately.

Editor's note: This lamb loin with a mellow garlic cream is served with deep-fried lamb ravioli in a dish that combines French and Asian flavors.

Marlo Thomas

Among my fondest childhood memories are the hours spent in the kitchen with my sister and my mother. My Italian mother is a phenomenal cook, and she would teach us how to prepare the dishes her mother had taught her. I remember the fun my sister and I had helping slice and dice, and the smell of the garlic sautéing in olive oil. ¶ When I moved out on my own, I would amaze people with this recipe for veal Marsala that my mother taught me to make when I was a little girl. Everyone thought I was a culinary genius. And the truth is that this recipe is simple to do. I hope you enjoy it.

VEAL MARSALA

¼ cup all-purpose flour

4 boneless veal cutlets
(10 ounces total)

2 tablespoons unsalted butter,
plus more as needed

2 tablespoons olive oil

8 ounces dried pasta

8 ounces white button
mushrooms, sliced

1 medium onion, chopped

1 garlic clove, minced

¾ cup water

2 tablespoons sweet Marsala wine

2 tablespoons dry Marsala wine

½ teaspoon salt

Ground white pepper to taste

SERVES

2

preparation

Preheat the oven to 150 degrees F. Put the flour in a shallow bowl. Dredge the veal in the flour until it is completely coated. Shake off any excess flour.

In a sauté pan or skillet large enough to hold all the veal cutlets in a single layer, melt the butter with the oil over medium heat. Add the veal and brown on both sides. Transfer the cutlets to a plate, and cover with aluminum foil (reserve the pan with the drippings). Keep the veal warm in the oven.

In a large pot, bring water to a boil over high heat. Cook the pasta according to package directions until al dente. Drain the pasta in a colander, return it to the pot, and cover.

In the pan containing the drippings, sauté the mushrooms, onion, and garlic over medium heat for 2 minutes. Add more butter if the mixture becomes too dry. Stir in the water, Marsala wines, salt, and white pepper. Simmer, uncovered, over low heat for 5 minutes, or until the sauce thickens.

Transfer the pasta to a serving platter. Arrange the veal on top and spoon the mushroom sauce over the dish. Serve immediately.

Tommy Tune

We never ate traditional breakfasts in Texas. My favorite was meat loaf, cheese toast, a Dr. Pepper and some of last night's gravy over last night's leftover mashed potatoes. Those were the best mornings.

preparation

Preheat the oven to 200 degrees F. In a large cast-iron skillet, heat the oil over medium heat. Add the ham and brown lightly on one side then the other, about 5 to 7 minutes per side. With a metal spatula, transfer the ham from the skillet to a cutting board and cut into quarters. Place the ham on a serving plate. Cover with aluminum foil and place in the oven to keep warm.

Whisk the flour into the drippings in the skillet. Continue to whisk over medium heat until the mixture is pale brown. Add the remaining ingredients and whisk until smooth; continue whisking until the gravy thickens enough to coat the back of a spoon.

Discard the bay leaf and pour the gravy over the ham. Accompany with mashed potatoes, if you like.

PAPA TUNE'S HAM AND RED-EYE GRAVY

1 tablespoon vegetable oil

One 1-pound country ham steak, ¼-inch thick

2 tablespoons all-purpose flour

1 cup canned beef broth

¼ cup bourbon

Hot sauce to taste

1 teaspoon dark brown sugar

1 bay leaf

Ground black pepper to taste

SERVES

2–4

THE CHICKEN'S REASON

POULTRY

Recently,

I suffered a blocked artery
and had to alter my eating habits.
Gone were the steaks and eggs
and in came the fish and chicken.

Well, there are just so many ways
to cook chicken
and Joy did them ALL–a number of times.
The one thing I never complain about
is her cooking.

She's great.

But a chicken breast,
NIGHT *after* NIGHT,
gets to be a challenge.

Regis & Joy Philbin

preparation

Rinse the chicken and pat it dry with paper towels. In a sauté pan or skillet large enough to hold all the chicken breasts in a single layer, heat the oil over medium heat. Add the chicken breasts and brown them on both sides. Reduce the heat to medium-low, cover, and cook for approximately 10 minutes, or until cooked through and tender. Using tongs, transfer the chicken to a serving plate and cover to keep warm.

. . . .

Add the garlic and onion to the same pan. Sauté over medium heat until the onion is translucent, about 2 minutes. Add the wine and continue to cook until the wine is slightly reduced, stirring occasionally. Add the ½ cup chicken broth and bring to a boil.

. . . .

In a small bowl, blend the cornstarch or flour with the 2 tablespoons chicken broth. Stir the mixture into the skillet. Add the mustard to taste and the capers and continue to stir until well blended.

. . . .

Spoon the sauce over the chicken breasts. Sprinkle with parsley and serve immediately.

JOY'S CHICKEN WITH MUSTARD SAUCE

4 boneless, skinless chicken breasts
1 tablespoon safflower, corn, or peanut oil
1 large garlic clove, minced
1 small onion, coarsely chopped
½ cup dry white wine
½ cup plus 2 tablespoons canned unsalted chicken broth
¼ teaspoon cornstarch or flour
½ to 1 tablespoon Dijon mustard
2 tablespoons capers, drained
1½ tablespoons minced fresh parsley

SERVES

4

'Enough is enough,' *I said.* 'I don't CARE anymore. *No more chicken!'*

But Joy found one more way *to make chicken and make it unforgettable.* She made a mustard sauce *that came from* HEAVEN. *No kidding,* *you're going to love it.* *It's enough to* save *your marriage,* renew *your interest in chicken,* *and* keep your arteries open, *too.*

Now what else do you want?

Warren & Theresa Littlefield

preparation

Rinse the chicken and pat it dry with paper towels. In a skillet large enough to hold all the chicken breasts in a single layer, heat the oil over medium heat. Add the chicken breasts and brown them on both sides. Add the crushed tomatoes. Stir in all remaining ingredients except the salt and black pepper. Cook, covered, for 45 minutes, stirring occasionally. Season with salt and black pepper. Simmer, uncovered, over low heat until the liquid has reduced by one fourth, approximately 30 minutes. Remove from heat and serve.

CHICKEN CACCIATORE

4 boneless, skinless chicken breasts, cut in half lengthwise

2 tablespoons olive oil

One 14½-ounce can crushed plum tomatoes

2 celery stalks, chopped

6 ounces white button mushrooms, stemmed and chopped

1 medium onion, chopped

10 black Greek olives, pitted and sliced

8 green Sicilian olives, pitted and sliced

1 large garlic clove, minced

1 cup canned unsalted chicken broth

¾ cup dry white wine

1½ tablespoons white wine vinegar

1½ tablespoons pine nuts

1 tablespoon capers, drained

1 tablespoon dried oregano

1 teaspoon red pepper flakes

Salt and ground black pepper to taste

SERVES

4

THIS·IS·THERESA'S·GREAT-GRANDMOTHER'S·RECIPE.·.
SHE·WAS·BORN·IN·SICILY·IN·THE·LATE·1800S.·.·.·.·.
IN·ITALIAN,·CACCIATORE·MEANS·'THE·HUNTER.'·.·.·.
THIS·DISH·WAS·COOKED·OUT·IN·THE·FIELD·AFTER·.·.·.
A·HUNT·WITH·ALL·THE·NATURAL·INGREDIENTS·FOUND·.
IN·THE·FIELDS·AND·FARMS.·OVER·IN·AMERICA,·.·.·.·.
CHICKEN·CACCIATORE·WAS·USED·FOR·FESTIVE·.·.·.·.·.
SUNDAY·OR·HOLIDAY·DINNERS.·WHILE·THIS·DISH·.·.·.
IS·COOKING,·THE·AROMA·WILL·FILL·YOUR·KITCHEN·.·.
AND·STIMULATE·EVERYONE'S·APPETITE.·.·.·.·.·.·.·.·.
THE·CACCIATORE·CAN·BE·SERVED·OVER·RICE·OR·.·.·.·.
PASTA·AND·ENJOYED·WITH·RED·WINE·AND·FRENCH·.·.·.
OR·ITALIAN·CRUSTY·BREAD.·BUON·APPETITO!·.·.·.·.·.

AFTER I
PREPARE THE
CHICKEN, I
USUALLY TAKE
SOME FRESH
SPINACH AND
ADD A
BIT MORE
OIL AND
GARLIC TO
THE SKILLET
AND COOK THE
SPINACH FOR A
FEW MINUTES.
IT WILL ABSORB
THE FLAVOR OF
THE CHICKEN
AND WINE
MIXTURE. THIS
DISH IS GREAT
WITH A BAKED
POTATO.

Vendela

COUNTRY FRENCH CHICKEN

4 boneless, skinless chicken breasts,
cut in half and lightly pounded
1 tablespoon olive oil
1 tablespoon minced garlic
1 tablespoon minced fresh tarragon
½ cup dry white wine
¼ cup fresh lemon juice
1 tablespoon lemon pepper

SERVES

4

preparation

Rinse the chicken and pat it dry with paper towels. In a skillet large enough to hold all the chicken breasts
in a single layer, heat the oil over medium heat. Add the garlic and tarragon, and sauté for 2 minutes.
Stir in the wine, lemon juice, and lemon pepper. Add the chicken breasts and sauté them on both sides
until opaque and cooked through, about 8 to 10 minutes. With tongs, transfer the chicken to a serving plate,
cover with aluminum foil, and set aside.

· · · · · · · · · · · · · · · · · ·

Simmer the sauce, uncovered, over medium heat until it thickens, about 3 to 5 minutes. Spoon the sauce
over the chicken and serve.

This recipe is not as rich as a traditional coq au vin.

Also, since roosters — usually used in this recipe — are rarely found in the market, chicken has been substituted. This recipe has the addition of a basic stock made with red wine. Coq au vin may be served with pasta, new red potatoes, or mashed potatoes.

Jean Banchet

preparation

Note: Remember that the chicken needs to marinate overnight.

Rinse the chicken and pat it dry with paper towels.

. . . .

To make the marinade, in a large shallow baking dish combine all the ingredients. Mix well. Add the chicken in a single layer and spoon marinade over each piece. Cover and refrigerate for 24 hours.

. . . .

The next day, transfer the chicken to paper towels and pat it dry.

. . . .

Strain the marinade into a medium bowl, discard the bouquet garni, and place the marinated vegetables in a large, heavy pot or Dutch oven. Over medium heat, cook the vegetables until tender. Stir in the tomato paste, garlic, and red wine marinade. Add the fresh bouquet garni and cook to reduce the mixture to a syrupy consistency, about 20 to 25 minutes. Stir in the chicken stock and add the chicken bones. Simmer, uncovered, for 45 minutes, or until about 6 cups of liquid remain. Remove from heat and discard the bones.

. . . .

In another large, heavy pot or Dutch oven, cook the bacon over medium-high heat until lightly browned. Using a slotted spoon, transfer the bacon to a side dish. Add the chicken and brown it in the bacon fat on all sides for about 20 minutes. Remove the chicken to a side plate and discard all but about 1 tablespoon of the fat left in the pot. Sauté the shallots for 1 minute. Return the chicken to the pan. Lightly sprinkle flour over each chicken piece and cook for 2 minutes. Add the brandy and ignite with a long match. Shake the pan until the flames subside. Add the wine mixture and season with salt and white pepper. Cover and simmer over low heat for 40 minutes, or until the chicken is cooked through.

. . . .

Meanwhile, in a small saucepan, combine the pearl onions, water to cover, salt and white pepper, sugar, and 1 tablespoon of the butter. Simmer, uncovered, over medium heat for 30 minutes, or until onions are golden. Set aside.

. . . .

In a medium sauté pan or skillet, melt 1 tablespoon of the butter over medium heat. Add the mushrooms and sauté for about 2 minutes. Set aside.

. . . .

When the chicken is done, transfer it to a serving bowl using a slotted spoon. Add the onions, mushrooms, and bacon to the serving bowl. Whisk the remaining 2 tablespoons butter into the sauce in the pot or Dutch oven, strain it, and pour it over the chicken. Sprinkle with the parsley and serve immediately.

COQ au VIN

Two 2¼-pound chickens,
each cut into 8 pieces
Marinade
2 carrots, peeled and diced
1 small red onion, chopped
2 celery stalks, chopped
4 garlic cloves, minced
1 bouquet garni: 1 fresh parsley sprig,
1 fresh thyme sprig, and 1 bay leaf
tied together in cheesecloth
6 cups red wine

1 tablespoon tomato paste
2 garlic cloves, minced
1 bouquet garni: 1 fresh parsley sprig,
1 fresh thyme sprig, and 1 bay leaf
tied together in cheesecloth
8 cups chicken stock
1 pound chicken bones
5 ounces bacon, cut into small strips
1 tablespoon minced shallots
2 tablespoons all-purpose flour
3 tablespoons brandy
Salt and ground white pepper to taste
24 white pearl onions, peeled
1 teaspoon sugar
4 tablespoons unsalted butter
6 ounces white button
mushrooms, sliced
1 tablespoon minced fresh parsley

SERVES

8

Joe Theismann

WHEN I WAS GROWING UP IN NEW JERSEY, MY MOM WOULD MAKE THIS DISH FOR ME IF I DID WELL IN SCHOOL OR HAD A GOOD BASEBALL OR FOOTBALL GAME. THERE WERE ALSO TIMES IN MY ADULT LIFE WHEN THINGS WEREN'T GOING WELL, AND IF I VISITED MY MOM SHE WOULD COOK HUNGARIAN CHICKEN PAPRIKASH. SHE ALWAYS KNEW THERE WAS A WAY TO MAKE ME SMILE.

HUNGARIAN CHICKEN PAPRIKASH

One 3-pound chicken, cut into 8 pieces

¼ cup vegetable oil

1 medium onion, finely chopped

2 teaspoons salt

½ teaspoon ground black pepper

2 tablespoons sweet Hungarian paprika

½ cup plus 3 tablespoons water

1½ cups long-grained white rice

3 tablespoons all-purpose flour

¼ cup sour cream

SERVES

4

preparation

Rinse the chicken and pat it dry with paper towels. In a heavy sauté pan or skillet large enough to hold all the chicken in a single layer, heat the oil over medium heat. Add the onion and sauté until translucent, about 2 minutes. Add the chicken and brown on both sides.

• • • • • • • • •

In a small bowl, mix together the salt, black pepper, paprika, and the ½ cup water. Pour the mixture over the chicken. Cover and simmer over low heat for 45 minutes, or until tender.

• • • • • • • • •

In a medium saucepan, cook the rice according to package directions.

• • • • • • • • •

Remove the pan with the chicken from the heat, transfer the chicken to a side plate, and cover it with aluminum foil. Using a large spoon, stir the sauce in the pan, scraping up any browned bits on the bottom of the pan. Place the pan back on the stove over low heat.

• • • • • • • • •

In a small bowl, whisk together the 3 tablespoons water and the flour until smooth. Gradually whisk the flour mixture into the pan to thicken the sauce. Stir in the sour cream until well blended. Return the chicken to the sauce and simmer, uncovered, over low heat for 5 minutes.

• • • • • • • • •

Kathie Lee Gifford

SIMPLE SWEET-AND-SOUR CHICKEN

2 pounds boneless,
skinless chicken breasts

1 cup Russian dressing,
low-calorie if preferred

1 cup apricot preserves,
low-calorie if preferred

1 envelope onion soup mix

2 tablespoons water

1½ cups long-grained white rice

Optional

½ cup crushed pineapple, drained

½ cup sliced peaches, drained

¼ cup chopped green bell pepper

1 medium tomato,
seeded and chopped

½ cup broccoli florets, blanched

1 small carrot, peeled, sliced,
and blanched

SERVES

4

preparation

Preheat the oven to 350 degrees F. Rinse the chicken and pat it dry with paper towels. Place the chicken in a 9×12-inch baking dish.

. . . .

In a medium bowl, combine the Russian dressing, preserves, onion soup mix, and water. Stir with a wooden spoon until blended. Pour the sauce over the chicken. Cover the dish with aluminum foil and bake in the oven for 1 hour.

. . . .

Remove the foil and baste the chicken. If using the optional ingredients, add them now. Bake, uncovered, for an additional 30 minutes or until the chicken and vegetables are tender.

. . . .

Meanwhile, in a medium saucepan, cook the rice according to package directions.

. . . .

Transfer the rice to a serving platter. Arrange the chicken and fruits and vegetables, if using, on top of the rice. Spoon the sauce over the dish and serve immediately.

Some of my fondest memories consist of happy family dinners, cold weather, and a wonderful cozy fire in our fireplace.

Richard Meier

BARBECUED CHICKEN

12 pounds chicken pieces (breasts, drumsticks, thighs, and wings)

One 12-ounce can Coca-Cola

1 can frozen orange juice concentrate

1¾ cups ketchup, or 1½ cups chili sauce (or both)

1 tablespoon soy sauce

1 teaspoon Worcestershire sauce

2 garlic cloves, crushed

1 teaspoon ground ginger

½ teaspoon red pepper flakes

SERVES

12–16

preparation

Rinse the chicken and pat it dry with paper towels. Place the chicken breasts, skin-side down, along with the other pieces in two 10×15-inch baking dishes. Set aside.

....

In a large bowl, combine all the remaining ingredients. Stir until well blended. Pour the mixture over the chicken. Cover and refrigerate at least 1 hour, basting occasionally.

....

Prepare a charcoal fire in a grill or preheat a gas grill on high.

....

Remove the chicken from the marinade and reserve the sauce. Place the chicken skin-side down on the grill over medium-hot coals (the coals should look gray with an occasional red glow). If using a gas grill, reduce the temperature to medium. Cook approximately 10 minutes per side, or until the chicken is crispy outside and tender inside.

....

Meanwhile, pour the marinade into a medium saucepan and bring to a boil over high heat. Reduce heat to low and simmer, uncovered, for 5 minutes. Cover to keep warm.

....

Transfer the chicken from the grill to a large serving platter. Pour the sauce over the chicken or serve it on the side. Serve hot.

There are many fond memories associated with cooking and enjoying this barbecued chicken, so it is impossible for me to isolate just one. During the summer on the East Coast, I serve this chicken at least five or six times a season, and in Los Angeles even more frequently, weather permitting. I particularly like the flexibility of my recipe, as it allows you to improvise with ingredients and quantity depending on what you have on hand and who arrives unexpectedly.

Lynn Anderson

preparation

To make the salsa, preheat the broiler. Use a pastry brush to completely coat the tomatoes and Anaheim chilies with olive oil. Place them in a shallow baking pan and broil until charred. Transfer the tomatoes to a plate and the chilies to a small paper bag and close it. Set both aside to cool. Remove and discard the charred skin from the tomatoes and chilies. Seed and chop the flesh. In a medium bowl, combine the remaining salsa ingredients. Mix well and set aside.

· · · · · · · · · · · · · · ·

Preheat the oven to 350 degrees F. To make the filling, combine the chicken, onion, garlic, cilantro, sour cream, cheese, and cayenne pepper in a large bowl. Stir until well blended.

· · · · · · · · · · · · · ·

To make the sauce, combine the mushroom soup, milk, and cheese in a medium saucepan. Stir constantly over medium-low heat until the cheese has melted and the mixture is smooth.

· · · · · · · · · · · · · · ·

Using a pair of tongs, dip a single tortilla into the sauce until it is slightly softened. Transfer the tortilla to a plate and spread ½ cup of the filling in the center of the tortilla. Fold in the sides of the tortilla, roll it up, and place it seam-side down in a shallow baking pan. Repeat until all the tortillas have been used. Cover the tortillas with the remaining sauce. Bake for 20 to 30 minutes, or until bubbling hot.

· · · · · · · · · · · · · · ·

Serve the salsa alongside the enchiladas. Guacamole, sour cream, shredded lettuce, and grated Monterey jack and Cheddar cheeses are also nice accompaniments.

When I moved from California to Tennessee, there was no hint of the Mexican-influenced recipes on which I had been raised. It was a real culture shock!

I NEVER PROMISED

CHICKEN ENCHILADAS IN A CREAM SAUCE WITH NACHO MAMA'S SALSA

Nacho Mama's Salsa

3 large tomatoes

3 Anaheim chilies

¼ cup olive oil

3 to 6 jalapeños, seeded and minced

1 large onion, finely chopped

1 teaspoon minced garlic

¼ cup finely chopped fresh cilantro

Filling

1 cup shredded cooked chicken

1 medium onion, finely chopped

2 large garlic cloves, minced

½ teaspoon minced fresh cilantro

1 cup sour cream

2½ cups (10 ounces) grated Monterey jack cheese

½ teaspoon cayenne pepper

Sauce

One 10¾-ounce can condensed cream of mushroom soup

1 cup milk

1 cup (4 ounces) grated Velveeta cheese

12 corn tortillas

SERVES

6

I created this recipe
for **Julia Child**
on her *eightieth* *birthday.*

CHICKEN MOLD
WITH SAUTÉED
ARTICHOKES
AND POTATOES

3 medium globe artichokes

2½ tablespoons plus 2 cups corn oil

8 ounces white button mushrooms,
stemmed and thinly sliced

1 medium onion, thinly sliced

1 garlic clove, minced

3 to 4 fresh thyme sprigs, chopped

1 tablespoon minced fresh
Italian parsley

Salt and ground black pepper to taste

8 ounces chicken legs, skinned,
boned, and cut into pieces

3 medium Idaho potatoes

SERVES

4

Jean-Claude Parachini

preparation

Trim each artichoke stem to about ½-inch long. Wash the artichokes in salted water and drain, bottom up. Remove the thick, loose leaves around the base and cut off the tip of each remaining leaf with scissors. In a large saucepan half full with water, add a pinch of salt, cover, and bring to a boil over high heat. Place the artichokes in the saucepan and cover. Bring back to a boil and cook for 25 to 35 minutes, or until a leaf is easily removed. Remove from heat and drain in a colander, bottoms up, opening the leaves to release heat. Let cool.

....

Remove all the leaves from each artichoke, so that only a few layers of the pale, tender inner leaves remain. Cut each artichoke in half lengthwise. Remove the fuzzy choke, leaving only the heart, and chop the heart.

....

Preheat the oven to 350 degrees F. In a medium sauté pan or skillet, heat 1 tablespoon of the oil over medium heat. Add the mushrooms, onion, garlic, artichoke hearts, thyme, parsley, salt, and black pepper. Cook for 25 minutes, stirring occasionally. Set aside.

....

In another medium sauté pan or skillet, heat 1½ tablespoons of the oil over medium heat. Add the chicken and salt and black pepper to taste, and sauté for 10 minutes, or until tender. Set aside.

....

Peel the potatoes and cut them widthwise into ⅛-inch-thick slices. Pat the potato slices dry with paper towels.

....

In a large, heavy skillet, heat the 2 cups oil over medium-high heat. Gently fry the potatoes on both sides until they turn a very light golden color. Using tongs, carefully lift the potatoes out of the oil and transfer them to paper towels. Pat the potatoes dry to remove any excess oil. Repeat until all the potatoes have been cooked. Reserve 16 slices.

....

Line four 4×1⅞-inch ramekins with the remaining potatoes, overlapping the potatoes in a circular pattern. Divide the chicken and vegetable mixture among the ramekins. Cover each filled ramekin with 4 slices of the reserved fried potatoes.

....

Bake for 25 minutes, or until the top is golden and crispy.

....

Unmold the ramekins by placing an individual serving plate on top of each one and gently turning the plate over. Carefully lift off each ramekin. Serve immediately.

Joel Silver

JAPANESE TOREI CHICKEN

Course Number 1

2 pounds boneless, skinless

chicken breasts

4 daikons

(Japanese radishes), shredded

Soy sauce to taste

1 pound tofu, cut into

½-inch-thick slices

1 cup 2-inch-long slices

green onions (about 12)

Course Number 2

2 pounds ground chicken breast meat

2 large eggs

½ cup chopped green onions

(about 6)

Course Number 3

1 cup long-grained white rice

Broth created during the cooking

of the second course

SERVES

preparation

To prepare the ingredients for the first course, rinse the chicken and pat it dry with paper towels. Cut the chicken breasts into 1-inch cubes and place on a plate. Divide the grated radish and soy sauce among 4 individual bowls. Place the tofu and onions in separate containers.

· · · · · · · · · · · · · ·

To prepare the ingredients for the second course, in a medium bowl, combine all the ingredients. Shape into small balls approximately 1 inch in diameter.

· · · · · · · · · · · · · ·

In a large saucepan, cook the rice according to package directions.

· · · · · · · · · · · · · ·

To cook the first course, put half the cubed chicken, tofu, and sliced green onion into the pot of boiling water. Cook for 5 to 7 minutes, or until the chicken is tender. Using chopsticks, each person should remove a piece of chicken, tofu, and green onion and place them in a bowl with the radish and soy sauce mixture. Each bite should include a little radish, chicken, tofu, and green onion. When the first course has been completed, skim the foam from the cooking broth in the pot, season the broth with additional soy sauce, and immediately serve the broth as soup.

· · · · · · · · · · · · · ·

To cook the second course, start with a fresh pot of boiling water. Using chopsticks, each person should add a few meatballs to the water and cook them for 5 to 10 minutes or until they are tender and cooked through. The meatballs should be removed from the pot with chopsticks and eaten with any remaining radish mixture. Reserve the broth for the third course.

· · · · · · · · · · · · · ·

For the third course, divide the rice among 4 individual serving bowls. Add some of the reserved broth and season with soy sauce.

My favorite Japanese meal is from a little restaurant in Tokyo called Torei, whose specialty, and only entrée, is an unbelievable chicken dinner. I find myself thinking about this place frequently, but because its location is so far away, the next best thing is to make the meal yourself. It's not exactly the same, but if you close your eyes and dream of kimonos, anything is possible.

Set the room as if you are dining in Japan. place tatami mats (any kind of mat or big pillows can be used) on the floor around the hibachi to make the experience more comfortable. The hibachi should be filled with sumi charcoal – smokeless charcoal (regular charcoal must not be used indoors because its fumes are toxic)–and a big pot of boiling water should be placed on top. If you don't own a hibachi or have smokeless charcoal, an electric hot plate may be substituted. The feast can also be enjoyed outdoors.

The food is not cooked until the guests arrive. However, you will need to prepare for the three courses ahead of time. This dinner works best if each person cooks a small amount of food during each course. If you still want more, cook it while you are eating so it is ready when you are. The cooking and eating continues until each guest has had enough.

Cold sake is the recommended drink throughout the meal.

JOEL SILVER AS

JOEL

AN EPIC TALE
OF A MAN
AND THE MEAL
HE COULD
NOT LEAVE
BEHIND

JOEL SILVER PRESENTS A JOEL SILVER PRODUCTION
"JOEL" STARRING JOEL SILVER MUSIC BY JOEL SILVER EDITED BY JOEL SILVER DIRECTOR OF PHOTOGRAPHY JOEL SILVER
EXECUTIVE PRODUCERS MR AND MRS SILVER SCREENPLAY BY JOEL SILVER BASED ON A MEAL FROM THE TOREI, TOKYO
PRODUCED BY JOEL SILVER DIRECTED BY JOEL SILVER

Jill Larson

CHICKEN POT PIE

1 package (15 ounces) Pillsbury
refrigerated pastry pie crust
for a 9-inch pie (2 crusts included)

2 large carrots, peeled and diced

3 medium unpeeled new
red potatoes, diced

½ to 1 cup frozen green peas

2 teaspoons olive oil

12 pearl onions, peeled and halved

4 tablespoons unsalted butter

¼ cup all-purpose flour

2 cups chicken broth

½ cup heavy cream

2 teaspoons dried dill

⅛ teaspoon ground
nutmeg (optional)

Salt and ground black pepper to taste

1 cup cubed roasted chicken or turkey

1 large egg, lightly beaten

Paprika

SERVES

4–6

preparation

Preheat the oven to 350 degrees F. Prebake the pie crust for 10 minutes following
package directions. Place on a wire rack and let cool.

. . . .

In a medium saucepan, combine the carrots and potatoes and add water to cover.
Place over medium-high heat and cook for 5 minutes; add the peas and cook for an additional
2 minutes. Using a slotted spoon, transfer the vegetables to a large bowl.

. . . .

In a small sauté pan or skillet, heat the oil over medium heat. Sauté the onions until translucent,
about 2 minutes. Add to the vegetables.

. . . .

In a medium saucepan, melt the butter over medium heat. Gradually whisk in the flour,
mixing well. Whisking constantly, add the chicken broth, bring to a boil, and let boil for 1 minute.
Reduce heat to a simmer, and add the cream, dill, nutmeg, salt, and black pepper.
Continue to whisk until the sauce thickens enough to coat the back of a spoon.

. . . .

Add the chicken or turkey to the bowl of vegetables. Gently fold in the sauce until
well combined. Using a large spoon, transfer the mixture to the prebaked pie shell.
Place the top crust over the pie and pinch the edges together to seal. Using a pastry brush,
lightly glaze the top crust with the beaten egg and dust with paprika.

. . . .

Bake in the oven for 45 to 60 minutes, or until the inside is warmed through and the top crust
is golden brown.

. . . .

Transfer to a rack and let cool for 10 minutes before serving.

I grew up in Minnesota in the 1950s. My mother didn't get much pleasure from cooking. She preferred home improvement and decorating projects, so we ate many a Swanson's chicken pot pie. I loved them; a whole meal in a little pie tin! When I went to college, the freezer compartment in my apartment's refrigerator was filled with Fudgsicles and Swanson's pies. A couple of years later, I was living in Paris, dining on frog legs and pâté, melancholy for my beloved pot pies. In a moment of desperation, I 'invented' my own 'Larson's chicken pot pie,' and discovered how much better it was when made with fresh vegetables and freshly roasted chicken— such a hearty, comforting dish. I'd come a long way, baby! Now it is one of my specialties, requested by friends when they come over for dinner, or something I make on a winter's night when I want to feel cozy. I share it with you with much love, and I hope that it brings as much pleasure to you and your loved ones as it does to me and mine.

Daniel Leron

RECIPE PHOTOGRAPH ON PAGE 114

preparation

Rinse the hens and pat them dry with paper towels. Preheat the oven to 425 degrees F.

· · · · · · · · · · · · · ·

In a medium bowl, combine the bread, parsley, and thyme. In a small sauté pan or skillet, melt 2 tablespoons of the butter over medium-high heat. Add the bacon and fry until golden brown. Add the bacon and drippings to the bread mixture. Stir to combine.

· · · · · · · · · · · · · ·

Stuff each hen loosely with the bread mixture. Truss the guinea hens by tying cotton string to the ends of the drumsticks and bringing them close together. Using poultry skewers, attach the wing tips to the body of the bird. Rub 3 tablespoons of the butter evenly over each of the birds.

· · · · · · · · · · · · · ·

In a roasting pan large enough to hold both hens, place the birds on their left side and bake for 12 minutes. Baste and continue cooking for 5 minutes. Baste again and cook 3 minutes more. Turn the birds onto their right side and bake for 20 minutes, basting every 5 minutes. Finish by cooking breast-side up for 5 minutes, for a total cooking time of 45 minutes. Transfer the hens to a platter and cover to keep warm.

· · · · · · · · · · · · · ·

To make the sauce, pour off the fat from the baking pan and place the pan over medium heat. Add the wine and stir to scrape up the browned bits from the bottom of the pan. After deglazing, add the chicken stock and tomato. Cook to reduce by one-fourth. Add the remaining 3 tablespoons butter. Season with salt and white pepper. Cook to reduce to a syrupy consistency.

· · · · · · · · · · · · · ·

On 4 individual serving plates, arrange a breast and one leg. Pour sauce over each serving, garnish with a thyme sprig, and serve.

Editor's note: The technique used in this recipe for roasting the hens is a bit labor intensive, but will ensure a moist, evenly browned bird.

· · · · · · · · · · · · · ·

Fernand Point was the owner of a very famous restaurant in Vienne, France, called La Pyramide, where many great chefs went to train.

STUFFED GUINEA HENS FERNAND POINT

Two 1¼-pound Guinea hens

5 cups cubed white bread, dried overnight

⅔ cup chopped fresh parsley

Leaves from 1 fresh thyme sprig, minced

8 tablespoons (1 stick) unsalted butter at room temperature

4 bacon slices, diced

Sauce

¼ cup dry white wine

1 cup chicken stock

1 medium tomato, peeled, seeded, and chopped

4 tablespoons unsalted butter

Salt and ground white pepper to taste

4 fresh thyme sprigs

SERVES

4

Madeleine Kamman

A PLATE OF QUAIL FOR N'GAO

¼ teaspoon salt, plus salt for quail

18 fresh Chinese
long beans, stemmed

36 small yellow beets

36 small red beets

6 Thai lime leaves or other
deep green leaves

6 ginger blossoms or other blossoms

One 3×1-inch piece
fresh ginger, peeled

16 whole quail

6½ cups peanut oil

4 cups veal stock

Finely grated zest and juice
of one lime

13 garlic cloves, crushed

1½ tablespoons Szechuan
peppercorns, coarsely crushed

3 tablespoons dark soy sauce

1 tablespoon fino or other dry sherry

Salt and ground white pepper to taste

SERVES

6

*This recipe is dedicated to the memory of my friend N'Gao, who wore out
her skirts on the same French school benches as I did between 1942 and 1950.*

*N'Gao was a lovely Vietnamese girl whose mother was even lovelier.
It was this charming lady's exotic culinary talent that opened my young French mind
and palate to the haunting flavors of the Far East. Thanks to N'Gao, I discovered
fresh and candied ginger, spring rolls, and batter-fried shrimp.*

*The bright colors on this plate of quail remind me of the dazzling silk print gowns
that N'Gao and her mother wore daily.*

preparation

Fill a medium sauté pan or skillet half full with water and add the ¼ teaspoon salt. Bring to a boil over high heat. Add the beans and cook for 4 minutes. Using a slotted spoon, immediately transfer the beans to a medium bowl of ice water. Reserve the pan and water in which the beans were cooked. Drain the beans and transfer to a tea towel. Roll the beans in the towel and refrigerate until ready to use.

· · · · · · · · · · · · · · · · · ·

Cut off all but ⅓-inch of the beet greens to help prevent color loss. In the same pan of water used to cook the beans, cook the yellow beets about 20 to 30 minutes until fork tender. Using a slotted spoon, immediately transfer the beets to a medium bowl of ice water. Using the same pan of water, repeat the procedure with the red beets. Let the beets cool, then drain and peel. Remove the green tops and beet skin. Place the yellow and red beets in separate containers to prevent the color from leaching. Cover and set aside.

· · · · · · · · · · · · · · · · · ·

On a baking sheet, prepare 6 bouquets with one each of the chosen leaves and blossoms. Cover with plastic wrap and refrigerate until ready to use.

· · · · · · · · · · · · · · · · · ·

Place the ginger in a piece of cheesecloth large enough to grasp the ends when folded over. Using a meat mallet, crush and mash the ginger. Squeeze the cheesecloth and collect the juice in a small bowl. Reserve the ginger and juice.

· · · · · · · · · · · · · · · · · ·

Rinse the quail and pat them dry with paper towels. Cut 4 of the quail into quarters. In a sauté pan or skillet large enough to hold all the quail quarters in a single layer, heat 2 tablespoons of the oil over medium-high heat. Add the quail and brown well on all sides. Transfer the quail to a plate and reserve for another use. Pour off the oil from the pan. Place the pan over high heat, pour in the veal stock, and stir to scrape up the brown bits on the bottom of the pan. After deglazing the pan, bring to a boil. Reduce heat to low and simmer, uncovered, until the stock has reduced to about 1 cup. Pour the liquid through a fine-meshed sieve lined with cheesecloth into a small saucepan. Stir in ½ tablespoon

each of the ginger and lime juices, and half the lime zest. Cover and let steep.

· · · · · · · · · · · · · · · · · ·

Stuff the cavities of each of the 12 remaining quail with 1 crushed garlic clove and a large pinch each of salt and crushed Szechuan pepper.

· · · · · · · · · · · · · · · · · ·

In a small bowl, combine the soy sauce with the remaining ginger and lime juices, and the sherry. Using a pastry brush, completely coat each quail with the mixture.

· · · · · · · · · · · · · · · · · ·

Preheat the oven to 325 degrees F. Pour 6 cups of the peanut oil into a large saucepan and place over high heat until the oil registers 375 degrees F on a frying thermometer, and the oil is hot but not smoking. Add the quail, 3 at a time, to the oil, and fry, turning them as they cook, for 12 to 15 minutes or until coppery gold and cooked through. Using tongs, carefully remove the quail to a shallow baking pan. Repeat the process, cooking the remaining quail 3 at a time. Bake the fried quail in the oven for 8 minutes.

· · · · · · · · · · · · · · · · · ·

Cut 1 large slice from the reserved ginger. In a small sauté pan or skillet, heat the remaining 2 tablespoons oil over high heat. Add the ginger slice and remaining garlic clove, and fry for 1 minute. Using a slotted spoon, remove and discard the ginger and garlic. Reduce heat to medium, add the beans, and rewarm. Season with salt and white pepper. Using a slotted spoon, transfer the beans to a side plate and cover with aluminum foil to keep warm. Reheat the beets by tossing them in the same oil over medium heat for 2 minutes.

· · · · · · · · · · · · · · · · · ·

To assemble, arrange 3 beans on the side of each plate to form large overlapping circles. In each of the three spaces where the circles overlap, place 2 yellow and 2 red beets. In the center of the plate, place 2 quail, each facing in opposite directions. Place a leaf and blossom bouquet between the quail. Spoon 1 tablespoon of sauce onto each bird and serve immediately.

FISH

While working on a hotel project in the south of France, one of the workers, a bricklayer artisan, overheard our conversation, which, when not about Frenchwomen, was almost always about food and wine. This time, the subject was how to grill fish. In a thick Greek accent, he said, "I know a woman who can grill fish better than anyone!" We inquired about where this woman was and dreamed of a small deserted island in Greece. "Just down the beach, about a 10-minute drive from here," he replied. We asked, "Do you think we can try her fish sometime?" And the artisan responded, "If you have a couple of bottles of a nice Chablis, I'll see what I can do." With a knowing grin, he scribbled down an address on a piece of dirty paper.

Later that evening, with a case of Chablis in tow, we showed up at the doorstep of a humble fisherman's shack, where we were greeted by our host, the bricklayer, and his splendid wife surrounded by four beautiful children, and a magnificent olive oil aroma. We were introduced to the most spectacular grilled fish and pepper salad of our lives — and the Mediterranean was our witness.

NO.	DATE	DESCRIPTION		LEGEND

Adam D. Tihany

RECIPE PHOTOGRAPH ON PAGE 134

preparation

Prepare a charcoal fire in a grill, or preheat a gas grill on high. Add soaked
drained mesquite wood chips to the gas grill, if desired.

. . . .

Rinse the fish and pat dry with paper towels. In a small bowl, mix the olive oil,
lemon juice, capers, parsley, chives, basil, and garlic. Add salt and black pepper.

. . . .

On a cutting board, using a very sharp knife, score the fish on both sides at a 45-degree angle,
cutting a quarter of the way into the fish every 2½ inches. Completely coat the fish
with the olive oil mixture and place 2 sprigs of the thyme inside each fish.
Wrap each fillet entirely in grape leaves—about 5 to 6 leaves per fish—and secure them
around the fish with a piece of cotton string. Set aside.

. . . .

To make the grilled peppers with yogurt, preheat the broiler. Use a pastry brush
to completely coat the peppers with olive oil. Reserve the remaining olive oil for the pecans.
Place the peppers in a shallow baking pan and broil until charred and soft. Place the peppers
in a brown paper bag, close it, and let cool. Remove the charred skin from the peppers
and cut the peppers lengthwise into eighths. Set aside.

. . . .

In a small sauté pan or skillet, heat the reserved olive oil over medium-high heat.
Add the pecans and fry until they turn a dark golden brown. Remove from heat and,
using a slotted spoon, transfer the pecans onto paper towels and pat dry.

. . . .

In a small bowl, mix together the yogurt and salt. Spoon the mixture onto a serving plate.
Place the peppers on top of the yogurt and sprinkle with the pecans and mint.
Add the black pepper.

. . . .

If using a charcoal grill, sprinkle soaked drained mesquite wood chips over the coals if you like.
Place the fish on the grill over medium-hot coals (the coals should look gray with
an occasional red glow). If using a gas grill, reduce the temperature to medium.
Cover the fish with aluminum foil. Cook for 10 minutes per inch of thickness, turning once.
Remove from the grill.

. . . .

Using scissors, carefully remove the cotton string from around the grape leaves.

. . . .

Gently unwrap the top grape leaves to expose the fish. Transfer to a dinner plate.
Garnish with lemon wedges and serve immediately with the grilled peppers and yogurt.

GRILLED MEDITERRANEAN BASS IN GRAPE LEAVES AND GRILLED PEPPERS WITH YOGURT

4 Mediterranean bass or red snapper
fillets (about 8 to 10 ounces each)

½ cup olive oil

¼ cup fresh lemon juice

1 tablespoon capers,
drained and minced

2 tablespoons minced fresh parsley

2 tablespoons snipped fresh chives

2 tablespoons minced fresh basil

4 garlic cloves, minced

Salt and ground black pepper to taste

8 fresh thyme sprigs

24 large bottled grape leaves

Grilled Peppers with Yogurt

3 red bell peppers

½ cup olive oil

¾ cup pecans

3 cups plain yogurt

2 teaspoons salt

2 tablespoons chopped fresh mint

Ground black pepper to taste

1 large lemon, sliced into wedges

SERVES

4

FISH

137

Georges Blanc

preparation

To make the court bouillon, combine all the ingredients in a medium saucepan. Cover and bring to a boil over high heat. Reduce the heat to low and simmer, uncovered, for 30 minutes. Season with salt and white pepper. Pour the liquid through a fine-meshed sieve lined with cheesecloth into a medium bowl. Use the bottom of a sturdy ladle to force as much liquid through the strainer as possible. Set aside.

∙∙∙∙∙∙∙∙∙∙∙∙∙∙

Grease a sided baking pan large enough to hold the fish in a single layer. Rinse the fish and pat it dry with paper towels. Place the fish on the prepared pan. Season lightly with salt and white pepper. Set aside. Preheat the oven to 450 degrees F.

∙∙∙∙∙∙∙∙∙∙∙∙∙∙

To make the sauce, blanch the tomatoes in rapidly boiling water for 20 seconds. Drain and submerge in a bowl of ice water. When the tomatoes are cool, remove the skin and seeds, and dice. Set aside.

∙∙∙∙∙∙∙∙∙∙∙∙∙∙

Place a medium sauté pan or skillet over medium-high heat and add the 7 tablespoons of oil. Reduce the heat to medium and add the shallots. Sauté for 1 minute. Stir in the tomatoes and court bouillon to obtain a fairly thick sauce. Season with salt and white pepper. Add the ground thyme flowers and bay leaf, and ½ tablespoon of the lemon juice. Cook the sauce for approximately 8 minutes to reduce it by one-fourth.

∙∙∙∙∙∙∙∙∙∙∙∙∙∙

Meanwhile, in a small saucepan, combine the water and the remaining 3 tablespoons of lemon juice. Bring to a boil over high heat. Using a wire whisk, mix in the butter 1 tablespoon at a time until smooth. Remove from heat.

∙∙∙∙∙∙∙∙∙∙∙∙∙∙

As soon as the tomato mixture has reduced, remove from heat and season with salt and white pepper to taste. Whisk in three-fourths of the melted butter mixture along with the basil, chives, and tarragon. The sauce should be thick enough to coat the back of a spoon. Adjust the consistency, if necessary, with more olive oil, court bouillon, and the remaining butter mixture. Whisk briskly to obtain a smooth sauce.

∙∙∙∙∙∙∙∙∙∙∙∙∙∙

Just before serving, lightly sprinkle the fish with water and bake in the oven for 2 to 3 minutes or until opaque throughout. Watch closely and remove from the oven as soon as the fish is cooked through.

∙∙∙∙∙∙∙∙∙∙∙∙∙∙

Using a metal spatula, transfer the fillets to the center of 4 serving plates. Generously spoon the sauce over the bass and garnish each serving with 3 chervil sprigs. Serve immediately.

Editor's note: This is the perfect dish for a garden luncheon. Serve on individual plates surrounded by a colorful array of spring vegetables. A basket of crusty French bread and sweet butter can accompany this delicious entrée.

BASS WITH FRESH HERBS AND EXTRA VIRGIN OLIVE OIL

Court Bouillon

2 carrots, peeled and thickly sliced

1 medium onion, quartered

4 medium shallots, halved

1 stalk celery, coarsely chopped

2 garlic cloves, halved

1 large lemon, peeled and halved

½ bay leaf

1 fresh thyme sprig

1 bunch fresh parsley

1¾ cups dry white wine

1 cup water

Salt and ground white pepper to taste

4 bass fillets (8 ounces each, ¼-inch thick)

Salt and ground white pepper to taste

Sauce

2 large tomatoes

7 tablespoons olive oil, plus more as needed

3 medium shallots, chopped

1 cup court bouillon, above

Salt and ground white pepper to taste

12 fresh thyme flowers and half a bay leaf, ground in a mortar

3½ tablespoons fresh lemon juice

¼ cup water

½ cup (1 stick) unsalted butter, cut into tablespoon-sized pieces

1 tablespoon chopped fresh basil

1 tablespoon snipped fresh chives

1 tablespoon chopped fresh tarragon

12 fresh chervil sprigs

SERVES

4

Rose Tarlow

CRABMEAT CASSEROLE

6 medium eggs

½ cup medium-grained white rice

2 cups (about 10 ounces)
fresh lump crabmeat,
rinsed and picked over

1 cup mayonnaise or more as needed

1 cup (4 ounces) grated
Parmesan cheese

1 large onion, finely chopped

SERVES

4

preparation

Put the eggs in a medium saucepan, cover with cold water,
and bring to a boil over high heat. Reduce heat to low, and simmer for
10 minutes. Remove the pan from heat and run cold water over the eggs until they are
cool to the touch. Shell the eggs, and chop. Place in a large bowl and set aside.

. . . .

In a medium saucepan, cook the rice according to package directions.

. . . .

Preheat the oven to 350 degrees F. Grease an 8-inch round casserole.

. . . .

In a large bowl, combine the rice with the eggs and stir in the remaining ingredients.
The mixture should be fairly moist. If not, add more mayonnaise.
Spoon the mixture into the prepared casserole dish. Bake in the oven for 45 minutes,
or until golden brown and bubbly. Serve hot.

*I've been making this recipe
since I was seventeen, and it's always
gotten rave reviews.
It's also easy and pretty foolproof!*

James Earl Jones

preparation

In a large sauté pan or skillet, melt the butter over medium heat. Add the onions and sauté until caramelized, about 45 to 60 minutes. In a blender, combine the cooked onions, tomatoes, shallots, garlic, and basil. Blend on medium speed until coarsely puréed.

. . . .

Preheat the oven to 425 degrees F. In a large sauté pan or skillet, heat the olive oil over low heat. Add the onion purée. Cook for 30 minutes, stirring occasionally. If the mixture gets too thick, gradually add the chicken broth.

. . . .

Rinse the sea bass and pat it dry with paper towels. Season with salt and white pepper. Place the sea bass in a rectangular baking dish large enough to hold all the fish in a single layer. Place the onion-and-tomato purée on top and bake in the oven for 15 to 20 minutes, or until the fish is opaque and cooked through.

. . . .

Place 2 pieces of sea bass on each of 6 serving plates. Spoon the purée over the fish. Serve immediately.

Editor's note: The chunky onion-and-tomato purée is the perfect topping for this firm yet delicate-tasting fish.

CHILEAN SEA BASS

½ cup (1 stick) unsalted butter

10 Maui or other sweet white onions, sliced

12 fresh plum tomatoes, seeded and chopped, or one 28-ounce can plum tomatoes, drained and chopped

4 large shallots, chopped

3 garlic cloves, minced

3 fresh basil leaves, chopped

1 tablespoon extra virgin olive oil

About ½ cup canned unsalted chicken broth

Twelve 2 × 2½-inch pieces Chilean sea bass

Salt and ground white pepper to taste

SERVES

6

FISH

141

Jim Palmer

ORANGE ROUGHY OREGANATA

4 medium (about 6 ounces each)
orange roughy, grouper,
or red snapper fillets

⅔ cup seasoned Italian bread crumbs

⅓ cup grated Parmesan cheese

1 tablespoon dried oregano

2 tablespoons unsalted butter, melted

Juice of 1 medium lemon

4 lemon slices

1 tablespoon minced fresh parsley

SERVES

4

preparation

Preheat the oven to 350 degrees F. Grease a 9×12-inch baking dish. Rinse the fillets and pat them dry with paper towels.

. . . .

In a small bowl, combine the bread crumbs, Parmesan, and oregano. Mix to blend. Using your hands, completely coat the fillets with the mixture, and place them in the baking dish. Drizzle the butter, then the lemon juice, over the fillets.

. . . .

Bake for 15 minutes, or until cooked through. Remove the fish from the oven. Immediately set the oven to broil and place the rack approximately 5 inches from the broiler. Place the fish under the broiler and broil until the bread crumbs are evenly browned, about 30 seconds.

. . . .

Transfer the fish to a serving plate. Garnish with lemon slices and parsley. Serve immediately.

JIM PALMER

I played baseball for the Baltimore Orioles for twenty years, and during our spring training in Florida I enjoyed eating this entrée at my favorite restaurant in Coconut Grove.

Kathy Mattea

preparation

Prepare a charcoal fire in a grill or preheat a gas grill on high. Add soaked drained mesquite wood chips to the gas grill if desired. Rinse the fish steaks and pat them dry with paper towels. Set aside.

....

To make the peppercorn butter, combine the bread crumbs, butter, shallot, parsley, Szechuan and black peppercorns, and garlic in a food processor fitted with a steel blade, or a blender. Process until the peppercorns are coarsely ground. Add salt and black pepper and pulse 3 times.

....

To make the sour cream sauce, combine the sour cream, wine, lemon juice, and white peppercorns in a small bowl. Mix until well blended. Add salt and black pepper. Cover and set aside.

....

Preheat the broiler. Cover both sides of the salmon with some of the peppercorn butter. If using a charcoal grill, sprinkle drained soaked mesquite wood chips over the coals if you like. Place the fish on the grill over medium-hot coals (the coals should look gray with an occasional red glow). If using a gas grill, reduce the temperature to medium. Cook for 3½ minutes on each side.

....

Transfer the salmon from the grill to a broiler pan. Coat the fish with more peppercorn butter and broil until crusty, about 1 to 2 minutes. Transfer the salmon to a serving plate and serve immediately with the sour cream sauce.

This is one of my favorite ways to serve fish. Try it, you'll like it!

PEPPERED SALMON

Six 6-ounce salmon steaks, about 1-inch thick

Peppercorn Butter

1 cup dried white bread crumbs

1 cup (2 sticks) unsalted butter at room temperature

1 large shallot, minced

1 tablespoon minced fresh parsley

2 tablespoons Szechuan peppercorns

2 tablespoons black peppercorns

2 teaspoons minced garlic

Salt and ground black pepper to taste

Sour Cream Sauce

2 cups sour cream

½ cup dry white wine

6 tablespoons fresh lemon juice

3 tablespoons white peppercorns, cracked

Salt and ground black pepper to taste

SERVES

6

This dish is wonderful with crusty peasant bread and a crisp Sauvignon Blanc or a white wine from Provence.

Charles Palmer

preparation

Place the cod on a cutting board and cut it into four 1-inch-wide crosswise strips. Roll up the pieces into 4 equal roulades. Carefully wrap each roll with 1 piece of Parma ham. Tie each roll with cotton string, then transfer them to a plate and set aside.

· · · · · · · · · · · · · · ·

Place the potatoes in a large saucepan, cover with cold water, and add the 1 tablespoon salt. Bring the potatoes to a boil over high heat, reduce heat to medium low, and simmer, uncovered, about 20 to 30 minutes, or until tender. Drain the potatoes in a colander and transfer to a food mill or ricer. Pass the potatoes into a large bowl, drizzle them with the olive oil, and season with salt and white pepper. Using a wooden spoon, stir the potato mixture until it is well mixed, yet fluffy and light. Cover with aluminum foil and set aside.

· · · · · · · · · · · · · · ·

Preheat the oven to 350 degrees F.

· · · · · · · · · · · · · · ·

Using paper towels, dry the cod rolls and season them with salt and white pepper. In a large nonstick sauté pan or skillet, heat the safflower oil over high heat until it begins to smoke. Using a spatula, place the rolls in the hot pan and sear until golden brown and crusty on all sides, turning carefully so they do not fall apart. Place a tiny piece of butter on each cod roll, and transfer them to a roasting pan. Reserve the sauté pan with the juices.

· · · · · · · · · · · · · · ·

Bake the cod in the oven for 5 minutes. Transfer the cod to a plate and cover with aluminum foil to keep warm.

· · · · · · · · · · · · · · ·

To make the sauce, blanch the tomato in rapidly boiling water for 20 seconds, drain, and submerge in a bowl of ice water. When the tomato is cool, remove the skin and seeds, and dice.

· · · · · · · · · · · · · · ·

Add the diced tomato, olive oil, vinegar, olives, parsley, and stock to the juices in the reserved pan and bring to a boil over high heat, stirring constantly. Reduce heat to low and simmer, uncovered, until the sauce is reduced by half. Season with salt and black pepper. Transfer the artichoke quarters to the pan and cook over low heat for 2 minutes or until warm.

· · · · · · · · · · · · · · ·

To serve, place a large spoonful of potato purée in the center of each of 4 serving plates. Carefully remove the string from each cod roll and place one roll on top of each spoonful of potato purée. Place 8 artichoke quarters around the perimeter of the plates and spoon the sauce over the top of the cod, potato purée, and artichokes. Serve immediately.

PAN-ROASTED COD WITH PARMA HAM

One 1½-pound fresh cod fillet
(about 1 inch thick)
4 very thin slices Parma ham
2 pounds new red potatoes,
peeled and cut into slices
1 tablespoon salt, plus salt to taste
3 tablespoons olive oil
Ground white pepper to taste
3 tablespoons safflower oil
2 tablespoons unsalted butter
Sauce
1 medium tomato
½ cup extra virgin olive oil
3 tablespoons white wine vinegar
¼ cup coarsely chopped pitted
Niçoise olives
1 tablespoon coarsely chopped
fresh Italian parsley
¼ cup chicken stock
Salt and ground black pepper to taste
8 baby artichokes, blanched,
trimmed, and quartered

SERVES

4

When I think of this dish, I think of a perfect day in the Hamptons. I would wake up early, spend the morning riding and training my horses, and spend the afternoon working in the rose garden, taking a break for lunch and a book in between. I think of small dinner parties and lunches for our closest friends or weekend guests. Everything is grilled in the summer, because we like very relaxed cooking. Dining is informal and very often last-minute. Simplicity is the motto. Even for dinner parties, we don't get fancy.

KK

Calvin & Kelly Klein

preparation

To prepare the shrimp, mix the lemon juice, garlic, salt, and black pepper in a large bowl. Add the shrimp and refrigerate for 1 hour. Clean and cut the vegetables to individual serving sizes.

· · · · · · · · · · · · · ·

Prepare a charcoal fire in a grill or preheat a gas grill to high, then lower the temperature to medium before cooking.

· · · · · · · · · · · · · ·

If using red potatoes, parboil them first by putting the potatoes in a large saucepan with water to cover. Bring to a boil over high heat, reduce to a simmer, and cook for 10 to 12 minutes. If using sweet potatoes, parboil them 15 to 18 minutes. Remove saucepan from heat, drain the potatoes and pat dry. Cut potatoes into ½-inch thick slices before grilling.

· · · · · · · · · · · · · ·

Brush all the vegetables thoroughly with olive oil. Sprinkle with sea salt and black pepper. The cooking time will vary depending on the intensity of the heat, the distance of the rack from the coals, and the density of the vegetables. If cooking over medium-hot coals, for most vegetables plan on approximately 4 minutes on the first side and 3 minutes on the second side. Check the vegetables frequently, occasionally brushing with the olive oil. Cook only until just tender, because overcooked vegetables will fall apart.

· · · · · · · · · · · · · ·

When vegetables are almost done, remove the shrimp from the marinade and add to the grill. Cook for 2 to 3 minutes on each side, or until pink.

· · · · · · · · · · · · · ·

Transfer the shrimp and vegetables to a serving plate. Garnish with lemon wedges and serve.

GRILLED JUMBO
SHRIMP WITH
FRESH LEMON
JUICE AND
GARLIC, WITH
GRILLED
VEGETABLES

Shrimp

8 to 12 tablespoons fresh lemon juice

10 garlic cloves, minced

Salt and ground black pepper to taste

2½ pounds jumbo shrimp, peeled and deveined

Vegetables

2 pounds fresh seasonal vegetables such as asparagus, carrots, corn on the cob, eggplant, fennel, garlic heads, leeks, mushrooms, bell peppers, red onions, new red potatoes, sweet potatoes, summer squash, tomatoes, and zucchini

½ cup olive oil

Sea salt and ground black pepper to taste

1 large lemon, cut into wedges

SERVES

4

Mimi London

preparation

Prepare your campfire or charcoal grill to the hot-ember, low-flame stage, or preheat a gas grill on high and add some soaked drained mesquite wood chips.

. . . .

Rinse the fillets and pat them dry with paper towels. Brush each side of the fillets lightly with the oil.

. . . .

On a very hot grill 6 to 8 inches from the fire, place the trout skin-side down. Cook for 2 to 3 minutes on each side. Transfer the fish to a side plate. Remove and discard the skin.

. . . .

In a large, heavy iron skillet, melt the butter over the fire. Add the shallots and sauté until translucent, about 2 minutes. Pour in 1 cup of the champagne and cook until reduced by half. Add salt and white pepper, then the cooked trout, and heat thoroughly.

. . . .

Remove from heat and serve immediately with the remaining champagne.

MIMI'S
GREAT BEAR
WILDERNESS
TROUT

══════

2 medium (8 ounces each)
trout fillets, skin on
1 tablespoon vegetable oil
2 tablespoons plus 2 teaspoons
unsalted butter
3 large shallots, minced
1 bottle champagne
Salt and ground white pepper to taste

SERVES

2

WHEN YOU'RE TWO DAYS

OUT IN THE WILDERNESS

CAMPED NEXT TO A TRULY PURE

MONTANA MOUNTAIN RIVER,

AND YOU'VE HAD PACKHORSES

BRING THE IRON SKILLET AND CHAMPAGNE,

AND THE COWBOY YOU'RE WITH

IS A GOOD FLY FISHERMAN,

AND YOU HAVE A NICE COLD RIVER

TO CHILL YOUR CHAMPAGNE IN,

THIS ENTRÉE DOESN'T NEED ANY EMBELLISHMENT.

René Verdon

This recipe illustrates my fondness for fresh seafood. It is based on items that are found throughout the entire year and is simple to follow.

SEA SCALLOPS WITH ORANGE AND SAFFRON

1 pound sea scallops

Grated zest of 1 medium navel orange

½ cup fresh orange juice

1 medium tomato, peeled, seeded, and diced

½ teaspoon saffron threads

Salt and ground white pepper to taste

1 teaspoon unsalted butter

1 large shallot, minced

2 tablespoons dry white wine

¼ cup heavy cream

1 pound dried linguini

2 tablespoons minced fresh parsley

SERVES

4

preparation

Rinse the scallops and pat them dry with paper towels. On a cutting board, using a sharp knife, cut each scallop into 3 crosswise slices, and place them in a medium bowl. Add the orange zest, orange juice, tomato, saffron, salt, and white pepper. Cover and refrigerate for 3 to 4 hours. Using a slotted spoon, remove the scallops from the marinade and place on a plate. Reserve the marinade.

....

In a large sauté pan or skillet, melt the butter over medium heat. Add the shallot and sauté until translucent, about 2 minutes. Add the scallops and sauté for 1 minute. Using a slotted spoon, transfer the scallops to a side plate. Whisk the reserved marinade, wine, and cream into the same sauté pan. Bring to a boil over high heat. Reduce heat to low and simmer, uncovered, for about 15 to 20 minutes, or until the sauce has reduced by half. Set aside.

....

In a large pot, bring water to a boil over high heat. Cook the linguini according to package directions until al dente. Drain it in a colander and transfer to a large serving platter.

....

Return the scallops to the sauce and bring to a boil over high heat for 1 minute. Arrange the scallops on top of the linguini. Spoon the sauce over the dish, garnish with parsley, and serve immediately.

FISH

150

Jean Joho

*My cooking
has been influenced
by classic French
as well as modern
and Italian cuisine.
My signature style
is characterized
by the freshest
and finest ingredients,
with an emphasis
on simplicity
and design.*

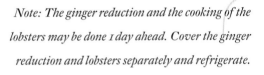

preparation

ROASTED
LOBSTER
WITH GINGER
AND ALSATIAN
GEWÜRZTRAMINER

Two 1½-pound live lobsters, or about
1 pound fresh-cooked lobster meat
3½ cups water
One 2½×1¼-inch piece fresh ginger,
peeled and julienned
2 tablespoons sugar
1½ cups Gewürztraminer wine,
preferably Alsatian
2 tablespoons olive oil
8 tablespoons (1 stick)
unsalted butter, cut into
tablespoon-sized pieces
1 pound fresh spinach,
washed and stemmed
Salt and ground white pepper to taste
1 tablespoon fresh lime juice
1½ tablespoons minced lime zest

SERVES

4

Note: The ginger reduction and the cooking of the lobsters may be done 1 day ahead. Cover the ginger reduction and lobsters separately and refrigerate.

If using live lobsters, fill a stockpot large enough to hold both lobsters three-fourths full of water and bring to boil over high heat. Plunge the live lobsters into the water, head first, and cover. Boil for 5 minutes. Transfer the lobsters to a large bowl of cold water. When cool enough to handle, drain the lobsters and set aside on a cutting board.

Put the water, ginger, and 1 tablespoon of the sugar in a medium saucepan. Bring to a boil over medium-high heat, and cook until the ginger is tender and the liquid has almost evaporated, about 45 minutes. Add the Gewürztraminer and boil until the liquid is reduced to 2 tablespoons, about 15 minutes. Set aside.

Preheat the oven to 425 degrees F.

If you have used live lobsters, remove the lobster tail and claw meat from the shells. Brush the lobster meat with the olive oil and transfer it to a large, heavy ovenproof sauté pan or skillet. Place the pan in the oven and roast the lobster for 10 minutes or until golden and firm. Transfer the lobster tails to a cutting board and the claw meat to a plate. Set aside.

Meanwhile, in another large sauté pan or skillet, melt 3 tablespoons of the butter over medium heat. Add the spinach and sprinkle with the remaining 1 tablespoon sugar. Sauté the spinach until it is wilted, about 4 minutes. Season with salt and white pepper. Divide the spinach among 4 individual serving plates.

In a small saucepan, heat the ginger sauce over medium-high heat. Gradually whisk in the remaining 5 tablespoons butter. Whisk in the lime juice and lime zest. Season with salt and white pepper to taste.

To serve, cut the lobster tails into slices on the diagonal. Fan the slices on top of the spinach and garnish with the claw meat. Drizzle the ginger sauce over the lobster and serve immediately.

GUILT

DESSERTS

With much love,
Elizabeth Taylor

What makes me happy? Holding my grandchildren. Just sitting with my children.

Playing with my puppies. Walking in the garden. Listening to the ocean.

It's not just one thing; it's a thousand little things combined that make me happy.

Oh, and my chef Neil's caramel ice cream and hot fudge sauce —

don't forget the caramel ice cream and hot fudge sauce.

Elizabeth Taylor

preparation

To make the ice cream, combine the Devonshire cream, heavy cream, and milk in a large saucepan. Warm over medium heat just until bubbles begin to form around the outer edge, but do not bring to a boil. Keep the mixture warm over low heat.

. . . .

In a large bowl, whisk the egg yolks lightly. Set aside.

. . . .

In a large saucepan over medium heat, combine the sugar and vanilla beans. Stir often until the sugar turns a uniform brown. Remove the pan from heat and submerge the bottom in a large pot or sink filled with 1 or 2 inches of cold water for about 30 seconds to cool slightly. Immediately whisk the resulting caramel into the cream mixture, one-fourth at a time. The cream will bubble and splatter, so be cautious.

. . . .

Reheat the mixture over medium heat, whisking constantly until all the caramel dissolves. Gradually pour approximately one-fourth of the mixture into the egg yolks, whisking constantly, then pour the egg mixture into the saucepan and whisk briefly to combine. Cook over low to medium heat, stirring constantly with a wooden spoon, until the mixture thickens enough to coat the back of the spoon. Strain through a fine-meshed sieve into a large bowl and whisk a few times to release the heat. Refrigerate to chill thoroughly, then freeze in an ice cream maker according to the manufacturer's instructions.

. . . .

To make the sauce, melt the chocolate and butter in a double boiler over barely simmering water. Remove the double boiler from the heat and set aside.

. . . .

In a medium saucepan, combine the sugar, corn syrup, water, and espresso powder.

. . . .

Bring to a boil over medium-high heat, whisking constantly. Boil for 1 minute, then remove the pan from the heat and whisk in the melted chocolate mixture and the heavy cream. Boil the mixture over medium heat until it reaches the degree of thickness you desire. Remove from the heat. If desired, stir in the liqueur.

. . . .

Serve the sauce warm or at room temperature over the ice cream. The sauce will keep for up to 6 weeks in the refrigerator.

NEIL'S CARAMEL ICE CREAM AND HOT FUDGE SAUCE

Caramel Ice Cream

2 cups Devonshire cream

1 cup heavy cream

1 cup whole milk

8 large egg yolks

1⅓ cups sugar

2 vanilla beans, split lengthwise

Hot Fudge Sauce

8 ounces semisweet chocolate (the better the chocolate, the better the sauce), chopped

3 tablespoons unsalted butter

⅔ cup sugar

½ cup light corn syrup

⅔ cup water

2 teaspoons instant espresso powder

2 tablespoons heavy cream

2 tablespoons Mandarin Napoleon liqueur (optional)

CARAMEL ICE CREAM

MAKES

1½ QUARTS

HOT FUDGE SAUCE

MAKES

2½ CUPS

This recipe comes from my dear high school friend Kelly Baker.
We both love to make this cake because not only is it truly delicious
(particularly the next day), but you can make it in no time at all.
The three-layer old-fashioned look makes it seem as if you've slaved
for hours. You'll fool everyone!

Julia Louis-Dreyfus

preparation

Preheat the oven to 350 degrees F. Grease and flour three 8-inch round cake pans.

· · · · · · · · · · · · · · ·

To make the cake, sift the flour, sugar, baking soda, baking powder, and cinnamon into a large bowl. Add the eggs and vegetable oil and stir until well blended. Fold in the grated carrots, pineapple, and pecans and stir until the mixture is thoroughly blended.

· · · · · · · · · · · · · · ·

Pour one-third of the batter into each of the prepared pans. Bake in the oven for 30 minutes, or until the edges have pulled away slightly from the pan and a toothpick inserted in the center comes out clean.

· · · · · · · · · · · · · · ·

Let the cakes cool in the pans for 15 minutes. Remove the cakes from the pans and let cool completely on wire racks.

· · · · · · · · · · · · · · ·

To make the icing, place the butter and cream cheese in a large bowl. Using an electric mixer set at medium speed, cream the butter and cream cheese until light and fluffy. Add the vanilla. Reduce the speed to low and gradually beat in the confectioners' sugar until smooth.

· · · · · · · · · · · · · · ·

Place a cake layer on a serving plate and frost the top. Repeat this procedure with the second and third layers. Finish by icing the sides of the cake. Cut into wedges to serve.

KELLY'S CARROT CAKE

Cake

2 cups unbleached all-purpose flour

2 cups granulated sugar

2 teaspoons baking soda

2 teaspoons baking powder

2 teaspoons ground cinnamon

4 large eggs, lightly beaten

1½ cups vegetable oil

3 cups grated peeled carrots (about 10 carrots)

One 8-ounce can crushed pineapple, drained

½ cup pecans, chopped

Icing

½ cup (1 stick) unsalted butter at room temperature

8 ounces cream cheese at room temperature

2 teaspoons vanilla extract

One 16-ounce box confectioners' sugar, sifted

MAKES ONE 8-INCH LAYER CAKE. SERVES 8–10

Alain Ducasse

preparation

PAN-ROASTED PINEAPPLE WITH **CRISP PASTRY** AND **CREAMED RUM** FROM **MARTINIQUE**

Puff Pastry

One 8-ounce puff
pastry sheet, chilled

¼ cup confectioners' sugar, sifted

Pastry Cream

½ vanilla bean, split lengthwise

1 cup whole milk

2 large egg yolks, lightly beaten

⅓ cup granulated sugar

4 teaspoons cornstarch

½ medium pineapple
(cut lengthwise), peeled

Sauce

6 tablespoons unsalted butter

10 tablespoons granulated sugar

3 tablespoons dark rum,
preferably from Martinique

¾ cup pineapple juice

1 cup heavy cream

12 large fresh mint leaves

SERVES

4

Lay out the puff pastry on a cool, dry work surface that has been sprinkled lightly with flour. Sprinkle the top side of the pastry dough lightly with flour. Using a rolling pin, roll out the puff pastry as thin as possible. Cut out four 6-inch-diameter circles and twenty 2-inch-diameter circles and release the air from the dough by pricking each circle several times with a toothpick. Place the circles on an ungreased baking sheet and freeze for approximately 30 minutes.

. . . .

Preheat the oven to 450 degrees F. Remove the baking sheet from the freezer and place another baking sheet on top of the circles to keep the dough from rising. Place the baking sheets in the oven and immediately reduce the temperature to 400 degrees F. Bake until the pastry begins to brown lightly, about 5 to 8 minutes. Remove the top baking sheet and continue baking until golden brown, about 5 minutes more.

. . . .

Remove the baking sheet from the oven, and lightly dust each pastry circle with confectioners' sugar. Preheat the broiler. Place the baking sheet under the broiler, about 30 to 45 seconds, or until the tops of the circles are golden brown. Be careful not to burn them. Place the baking sheet on a wire rack and let the pastry cool.

. . . .

To make the pastry cream, combine the vanilla bean and milk in a medium saucepan.

Place over high heat until small bubbles form around the edges of the pan. Set aside. In another medium saucepan, whisk together the egg yolks, sugar, and cornstarch until pale in color. Set aside.

. . . .

Remove and discard the vanilla bean and any skin that may have formed on the milk. Place the saucepan with the egg mixture over medium heat. Whisking continuously, slowly pour the milk into the egg mixture. Bring to a boil, reduce heat to low, and cook for 2 to 3 minutes, or until the mixture thickens enough to coat the back of a wooden spoon. Remove from heat.

. . . .

Cut a circle out of waxed paper large enough to cover and fit directly on top of the pastry cream. Butter one side of the waxed paper circle and place it on the pastry cream. Refrigerate until the cream is cool.

. . . .

Cut the pineapple into thirds lengthwise and cut out the core. Cut each third crosswise into ⅛-inch-thick slices.

. . . .

To make the sauce, combine 3 tablespoons of the butter and 5 tablespoons of the sugar in a large sauté pan or skillet. Cook over high heat, stirring occasionally, until the butter and sugar have turned a golden brown. Add half the pineapple slices and cook until well browned on both sides. Using a slotted spoon, transfer the browned pineapple pieces to a plate in a single layer. Pour the cooking liquid into a bowl and reserve. Repeat the process with the remaining 3 tablespoons butter and 5 tablespoons sugar, and pineapple.

· · · · · · · · · · · ·

Return all the reserved cooking juices to the pan, add 2 tablespoons of the rum, and ignite with a long match. Shake the pan until the flames subside. Cook the mixture over medium-high heat to reduce by half. Add the pineapple juice and cook again to reduce by half. Set aside.

· · · · · · · · · · · ·

Whisk the chilled pastry cream briskly to add volume. In a deep medium bowl, using an electric mixer set at highest speed, beat the heavy cream until stiff peaks form. Whisk one-fourth of the pastry cream into the whipped cream. Fold in the remaining pastry cream and the remaining 1 tablespoon rum.

· · · · · · · · · · · ·

To assemble, place a large circle of pastry in the middle of each of 4 dessert plates. Generously spread rum cream over each circle. Arrange a single layer of pineapple pieces on top of the rum cream. Overlap 5 of the smaller pastry circles in a circular pattern on top of the pineapple on each pastry. Place a dollop of rum cream in the center of each and decorate with 3 mint leaves. Finish by spooning some of the cooking juice around the base of each pastry and serve immediately.

This dessert is very **exotic**. It mixes crunchy and mellow t e x t u r e s as well as exotic flavors. It is a perfect **m i x** between the pineapple and **r u m**, which comes from **M a r t i n i q u e**. It has an **original** presentation and is one of my **f a v o r i t e** desserts.•••
This recipe **e x e m p l i f i e s** how I like to cook. It's made with simple ingredients and the result is **extraordinary**. For me, it is important to use the **b e s t** ingredients and make them as flavorful as possible.

Debra Ponzek

GROVE STREET BROWNIES

½ cup (1 stick) plus 2 tablespoons
unsalted butter

1½ cups sugar

¼ cup water

24 ounces semisweet chocolate chips
(the better the chocolate,
the better the brownies)

5 large eggs

1½ cups unbleached all-purpose flour

½ teaspoon salt

½ teaspoon baking soda

½ teaspoon vanilla extract

1 cup chopped walnuts

MAKES TWELVE
3-INCH BROWNIES

SERVES

12

*Jim Reed and Jerry Holmes were the
original owners of the Grove Street Cafe in
Greenwich Village. One of my earliest cooking
memories is of working with Jim and Jerry
at a dinner party. I hadn't even thought
of cooking as a career at this point, but later,
when I needed information about cooking
schools, I turned to them. They were
very helpful about schools and the profession
in general. I have wonderful memories of
going to the Grove Street Cafe with my family
and friends. They had a delicious lemon mousse
for dessert, and they served it with these
brownies. A perfect combination! They were
so good that I begged Jim and Jerry for the
recipe. They're still my favorite brownies.*

preparation

Preheat the oven to 325 degrees F. Grease and flour a 9×13-inch baking pan.

· · · · · · · · · · · · · · · · ·

In a large saucepan, combine the butter, sugar, and water. Bring to a boil over medium-high heat.
Reduce heat to medium, add half the chocolate chips, and stir constantly until melted.
Remove from heat.

· · · · · · · · · ·

While beating with an electric mixer set at lowest speed, add the eggs to the saucepan,
one at a time. Continue to beat until the mixture is well blended. Add the flour, salt,
and baking soda. Mix with a wooden spoon until smooth. Stir in the vanilla, walnuts,
and remaining chocolate chips. Pour the batter into the prepared pan.

· · · · · · · · · · · ·

Bake in the oven for 40 to 45 minutes, or until a toothpick inserted in the center of the brownies
comes out clean. The brownies should be slightly moist. Place the pan on a wire rack
and let cool completely. Cut into squares to serve.

Judith Light

My grandmother was a very beautiful woman inside and out. She was generous with her life and her cooking. She was an extraordinary person and an incredible baker. She'd be up by 5:00 A.M., baking bread, rolls, and cakes in her oven in the basement of her home in Scarsdale, New York. This was one of the cakes she would make. She'd make it not only for Thanksgiving, but for all kinds of holidays, as well as just any old time when people would come over for coffee and cake. My mother told me that at the bake sales, this would be the first cake to be sold. And sometimes Nana would bake it for a neighbor—just because. I like to think that her generosity of spirit and her creativity come through in this cake. Nothing has so connected me with love and support like AIDS has—so I now have a nice appreciation for what my grandmother was communicating to people through her baking when she didn't have the words.

Preheat the oven to 350 degrees F. Grease and flour a 10-inch round tube pan.

To make the filling, stir all the ingredients together in a small bowl. Set aside.

To make the cake batter, sift the flour and baking powder together into a large bowl. Set aside. Using an electric mixer set at the lowest speed, cream the butter and sugar together in another large bowl until light and fluffy. Add the eggs, one at a time, beating well after each addition. Stir in the vanilla.

In a medium bowl, combine the sour cream and baking soda. Using the electric mixer set at the lowest speed, alternately add the sifted dry ingredients and the sour cream mixture into the butter mixture one-fourth at a time. Beat until smooth.

Pour half the batter into the prepared pan. Sprinkle three-fourths of the filling on top. Add the remaining batter and top with the remaining filling. Run a knife through the batter to create a marbled effect, then smooth the top with a rubber spatula.

Bake in the oven for 1 hour and 15 minutes, or until a toothpick or cake tester inserted near the center of the cake comes out clean. Place the cake upside down on a wire rack to cool. To unmold, loosen the sides with a long metal spatula and remove the center core of the pan. Invert onto a greased wire rack and reinvert onto a serving plate.

Serve the cake warm or at room temperature.

NANA BESSIE HOLLANDER'S SOUR CREAM CAKE

Filling

1 cup chopped walnuts

½ cup sugar

2 teaspoons ground cinnamon

6 ounces semisweet chocolate chips, preferably minis

Cake Batter

4 cups unbleached all-purpose flour

4 teaspoons baking powder

1 cup (2 sticks) unsalted butter or margarine at room temperature

2 cups sugar

4 large eggs

2 teaspoons vanilla extract

2 cups (1 pint) sour cream

4 teaspoons baking soda

SERVES

12

Barry & CeCe Kieselstein-Cord

preparation

Preheat the oven to 325 degrees F. Grease and flour
a 10-inch bundt pan.

· · · · · · · · · · · · · · · · ·

In a large bowl, using an electric mixer set at the
lowest speed, cream the butter. Gradually add the
sugar and beat until smooth. Add the eggs, one at a
time, beating well after each addition. Keep
blending the butter mixture while alternately adding
the milk and flour, in fourths, beginning with the
flour. Beat until smooth. Add the vanilla, almond,
and butter flavorings, and mix until blended.

· · · · · · · · · · · · · · · · ·

Pour the batter into the prepared pan. Bake in
the oven for 1½ hours, or until a toothpick inserted
into the cake comes out clean. Place the cake on
a wire rack to cool. Cut into wedges to serve.

AUNT ANNE'S POUND CAKE

2 cups (4 sticks) unsalted butter
at room temperature

3 cups sugar

6 large eggs

¾ cup milk

4 cups cake flour

1 tablespoon vanilla extract

1 teaspoon almond extract

1 teaspoon butter flavoring

MAKES ONE
10-INCH CAKE.
SERVES
12

This recipe belongs
to my great-aunt.
Aunt Anne never had company
or family over without serving
her pound cake. I can still see her
in her kitchen in Louisiana baking up a
storm. Aunt Anne died at the age of 103—
still sharp as a tack and an amazing woman.

CECE KIESELSTEIN-CORD

Angela Cummings

preparation

Preheat the oven to 350 degrees F. Grease a 9-inch tube pan.

. . . .

To make the batter, sift the flour, baking soda, and baking powder together into a medium bowl. Set aside. In a large bowl, using an electric mixer set at lowest speed, cream the butter and sugar together until light and fluffy. Add the egg yolks, one at a time, beating well after each addition. Continue to blend the butter mixture while alternately adding the sifted dry ingredients and sour cream by thirds. Stir in the orange zest and walnuts or pecans.

. . . .

In a medium bowl, using an electric mixer set at medium-high speed, beat the eggs whites until stiff, glossy peaks form. Gently fold the egg whites into the batter with a rubber spatula. Pour the batter into the prepared pan.

. . . .

Bake in the oven for 50 minutes, or until the edges have pulled away slightly from the sides of the pan and a toothpick inserted near the center comes out clean.

. . . .

Meanwhile, to make the topping, stir the sugar, orange juice, and Grand Marnier together in a small bowl.

. . . .

When the cake is done, remove it from the oven, spoon the topping over the hot cake, sprinkle with almonds, and let it cool completely in the pan. Transfer to a serving plate and cut into wedges to serve.

All my best recipes come from friends,
because until I got married I very carefully avoided cooking!
Then, all of my friends came to my rescue,
especially Gene Moore, who is as good a cook as he is an artist.
He understood the need to keep it simple and wrote on the recipe:
"Now, dear Angela, here is another cake that even
an idiot can make — with great success! Even I can do it!"
Although my repertoire has since expanded,
this is still my favorite cake and traditionally has been
my husband's birthday cake every year.

GENE MOORE'S ORANGE CAKE

Cake Batter

2 cups unbleached all-purpose flour

1 teaspoon baking soda

1 teaspoon baking powder

1 cup (2 sticks) unsalted butter at room temperature

1 cup sugar

3 large eggs, separated

1 cup sour cream

Grated zest of 1 medium orange

½ cup chopped walnuts or pecans

Topping

½ cup sugar

¼ cup fresh orange juice

⅓ cup Grand Marnier

½ cup slivered almonds

MAKES ONE 9-INCH TUBE CAKE. SERVES 8

THIS RECIPE WAS PASSED DOWN FROM MY MOM,

AND IT IS MY 'VICE AFTER VICTORY.'

Pat Riley

preparation

Preheat the oven to 375 degrees F. Grease a 15½×10½-inch
sided baking pan. Line the pan with waxed paper,
grease the paper, and lightly flour it.
Chill a deep medium bowl in the freezer.

. . . .

Sift the flour, ¼ cup of the granulated sugar, the cocoa,
baking powder, and salt together into a medium bowl.

. . . .

In a large bowl, using an electric mixer set at
the highest speed, beat the eggs until foamy. Gradually add
the remaining ½ cup sugar and continue beating until thick
and pale in color. Stir in the vanilla. Using a spatula,
slowly fold the flour mixture into the eggs.

. . . .

Evenly spread the batter onto the prepared pan.
Bake in the oven for 10 to 12 minutes, or until the cake
springs back when touched in the center. Loosen the sides
of the cake with a knife and immediately turn the cake out
on a pastry cloth. Beginning at one of the narrow ends,
roll the cake and cloth together like a jelly roll.
Transfer to a wire rack to cool.

. . . .

To make the whipped cream, combine the cream, vanilla and
almond extracts, and granulated sugar in the chilled bowl.
Using an electric mixer set at the highest speed,
whip until stiff peaks form.

. . . .

Unroll the cake. Using a spatula, spread the
whipped cream evenly across the cake.
Roll up again without the pastry cloth.

. . . .

Carefully place the cake, seam-side down,
on a serving plate and dust with confectioners' sugar.
Refrigerate until ready, cut into slices, and serve.

RILEY'S ROLL

Cocoa Roll

½ cup sifted unbleached
all-purpose flour

¾ cup granulated sugar

¼ cup unsweetened
cocoa powder

½ teaspoon baking powder

¼ teaspoon salt

4 large eggs at room temperature

1 teaspoon vanilla extract

Almond Vanilla Whipped Cream

1 cup chilled heavy cream

1 teaspoon vanilla extract

¼ teaspoon almond extract

2 tablespoons granulated sugar

¼ cup confectioners'
sugar, sifted

SERVES

12

Karl Lagerfeld

APPLE STRUDEL

Dough

2 ¼ cups unbleached all-purpose flour

1 large egg, lightly beaten

½ cup plus 3 tablespoons water

Filling

⅓ cup raisins

3½ tablespoons dark rum

2 ¼ pounds (about 4 large)
Granny Smith or Cortland apples

3 tablespoons fresh lemon juice

½ cup granulated sugar

½ cup chopped, peeled hazelnuts

1 teaspoon ground cinnamon

¾ cup crème fraîche

¼ cup (½ stick) unsalted
butter, melted

½ cup heavy cream

Sifted confectioners' sugar

MAKES ONE
18-INCH-LONG STRUDEL.
SERVES

8

preparation

To make the dough, place the flour on a work surface and make a well in the center. Put the egg, a pinch of salt, and the water in the well. Work the ingredients together by first using a fork and then your hands, and knead until the dough becomes slightly elastic. Roll it into a ball, cover with a warm bowl, and let stand for 1 hour.

. . . .

To make the filling, combine the raisins and rum in a small bowl and set aside. Peel, core, and cut the apples into ⅛-inch-thick slices. Put the slices in a large bowl. Add the lemon juice and mix thoroughly. Add the sugar, nuts, cinnamon, and ½ cup of the crème fraîche. Drain the raisins and add them to the mixture. Stir the ingredients until they are well blended. Set aside.

. . . .

Preheat the oven to 400 degrees F. Generously butter a baking sheet.

. . . .

Place a very large pastry cloth over a work surface and sprinkle it with flour. Transfer the dough to the work surface. Using a rolling pin, roll the dough into a rectangular shape. Stretch as thin as possible (preferably paper-thin) without breaking it. Using a pastry brush, spread the remaining ¼ cup crème fraîche evenly over the dough. Spread the apple mixture over the dough, leaving a 1-inch border. Starting from one of the shorter sides, roll the dough up jelly-roll fashion, being careful not to roll it too tightly since the dough will expand while baking. Place the strudel seam-side down on the prepared pan. Using a pastry brush, coat the strudel with the melted butter.

. . . .

Bake in the oven for 20 minutes, or until the crust begins to brown. Brush with some of the heavy cream, and bake 20 minutes longer. Brush the strudel with cream again and bake for another 20 minutes, basting every 5 minutes, for a total baking time of 1 hour.

. . . .

Remove the strudel from the oven. Let sit on the pan for 5 minutes, then transfer to a serving platter. Dust with confectioners' sugar. Cut into slices and serve warm.

Apple strudel is one of my favorite dishes. I adore the scent of cinnamon, which brings back childhood memories of Christmas

L O

I'm lucky to have a w i f e who is a very good cook. What a pleasure it is to be s e r v e d by the person with whom you are in love. We enjoy this dessert on Sunday evenings in autumn.

V E

Pierre Gagnaire

preparation

To make the baked apples, preheat the oven to 300 degrees F. Grease one 12-inch sheet
of parchment paper or waxed paper and set aside. In a large saucepan, combine ¼ cup of
the water, the sugar, and ginger. Cook over medium heat, stirring often, until the sugar is a
uniform golden brown. Remove the pan from the heat. After 30 seconds, slowly whisk in the
remaining 3¾ cups water, 1 cup at a time. The syrup will bubble and splatter, so be cautious.

· · · · · · · · · · · · · ·

Place the apples in an ovenproof dish large enough to hold them in a single layer.
Pour the syrup over the apples and cover them with the buttered parchment or waxed paper.
Bake the apples in the oven for about 45 minutes, or until tender.

· · · · · · · · · · · · · ·

Baste the apples with their cooking liquid, then transfer them to a plate using a slotted spoon.
Pour the apple cooking liquid into a bowl and refrigerate until chilled. Return the apples
to the ovenproof dish, cover, and set aside.

· · · · · · · · · · · · · ·

To make the sorbet, stir the lemon juice into the chilled apple cooking liquid.
Freeze in an ice cream maker according to the manufacturer's instructions.

· · · · · · · · · · · · · ·

To make the poached plums, combine the honey, warm water, and the brandy
in a large saucepan. Bring to a boil over high heat. Reduce heat to low and add the plums.
Simmer, uncovered, stirring occasionally, for 15 minutes, or until tender. Using a slotted spoon,
transfer the plums to a plate and set aside. Reserve the poaching liquid in the pan.

· · · · · · · · · · · · · ·

To reheat the apples, preheat the oven to 350 degrees F. Rewarm the apples in the oven
for 20 minutes, or until heated through.

· · · · · · · · · · · · · ·

To assemble, return the plums to the saucepan containing the poaching
liquid and place over low heat to slightly warm the plums. Using a slotted spoon,
transfer 2 plums to each of 6 individual glass dessert bowls. Place a poached apple
and some sorbet on top of the plums in each bowl. Put an almond cookie in each bowl
and serve immediately.

GREENGAGE PLUMS AND PIPPIN APPLE COMPOTES WITH APPLE SORBET

Baked Apples

4 cups warm water

2 cups sugar

1 tablespoon minced fresh ginger

6 (about 2 pounds) small pippin
apples, peeled, cored, and left whole

Apple Sorbet

¾ cup fresh lemon juice
(about 4 lemons)

Apple cooking liquid, above

Poached Plums

½ cup lavender honey or other
mild-flavored honey

½ cup warm water

2 tablespoons white plum brandy

12 (about 2 pounds) greengage plums

6 crisp almond cookies

SERVES

6

Pierre Orsi

preparation

In a large nonstick sauté pan
or skillet, combine the butter and
sugar. Cook over medium heat,
stirring constantly, until
caramelized. Add the sliced apples
and cook about 3 minutes.
Pour in the rum and ignite
the mixture with a long match.
Shake the pan until
the flame subsides.

· · · · · · · · · · · · · · · ·

To serve, place 2 large
scoops of ice cream
in each of 4 individual
glass dessert bowls.
Arrange the apples on top
and spoon the cooking juice
over the apples and ice cream.
Serve immediately.

*Editor's note: This elegant dessert
is easy to prepare. Apple-lovers
will delight in the combination
of rum-flavored apples
and vanilla ice cream.*

APPLE DELIGHT
AND ICE CREAM

4 tablespoons (½ stick)
unsalted butter
¼ cup sugar
4 pippin apples, peeled, cored,
and cut into ¼-inch-thick slices
2 tablespoons dark rum
1 quart vanilla ice cream

SERVES

4

Roland Passot

preparation

To make the caramel sauce, combine the sugar and water in a large saucepan over medium heat. Stir constantly until the mixture is an even golden brown, about 15 minutes. Remove from heat and slowly whisk in the cream. The mixture will bubble and splatter, so be cautious. Add the butter and continue whisking until it has melted and the sauce is smooth. Set aside.

. . . .

To make the napoleons, preheat the oven to 500 degrees F. Grease 2 baking sheets. Lay a single sheet of phyllo dough on a cutting board and dust lightly with confectioners' sugar. Repeat the procedure with the remaining phyllo dough, layering the sheets on top of the first sheet. Cut out eighteen 5-inches circles. Sprinkle the tops again with confectioners' sugar, then mist the circles with water. Transfer the circles to the prepared baking sheets. Reduce the oven temperature to 450 degrees F and bake the circles in the oven until golden brown, about 10 minutes. Transfer the circles to a wire rack to cool.

. . . .

In a large sauté pan or skillet, melt the butter over high heat. Add the apple slices and sauté for 8 to 10 minutes, or until tender and a light golden color. Sprinkle the granulated sugar over the apples and continue cooking until golden brown. Using a slotted spoon, transfer the apples to a medium bowl. Add the Calvados or applejack to the pan, stir to dissolve the caramel that has formed, and cook over medium-high heat to reduce by half. Pour the liquid over the apples. Stir to combine.

. . . .

To serve, place a phyllo circle on each of 6 dessert plates. Arrange a layer of apples on top and cover with another phyllo circle. Repeat the procedure, finishing with a layer of phyllo. Dust the tops with confectioners' sugar and serve immediately with the caramel sauce.

COOKING FOR ME IS MORE THAN JUST RECIPES. IT'S A PLEASURE OF LIFE – PLEASURE THAT YOU GIVE FROM THE BOTTOM OF YOUR HEART TO THE TABLE WITH THE EYES, THE SMELL, THE FRAGRANCE, AND OF COURSE, THE TASTE AND FLAVOR. IT IS A PASSION AND A LABOR OF LOVE. BE PASSIONATE WITH YOUR COOKING, AND YOU WILL BRING YOUR GUESTS MANY UNFORGETTABLE MOMENTS!

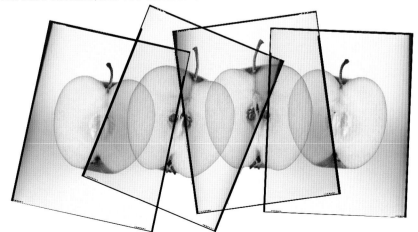

NAPOLEONS OF APPLE WITH CARAMEL SAUCE

Caramel Sauce
1 cup granulated sugar
½ cup water
1½ cups heavy cream
1 tablespoon unsalted butter at room temperature, cut into small pieces
Napoleons of Apple
3 sheets phyllo dough
Sifted confectioners' sugar
½ cup (1 stick) unsalted butter
3 or 4 Granny Smith apples, peeled, cored, and cut into eighths
1 cup granulated sugar
¼ to ⅓ cup Calvados or applejack
Sifted confectioners' sugar

SERVES

6

Michel Rostang

preparation

Preheat the oven to 375 degrees F. Line a baking sheet with parchment paper or waxed paper, then grease it. Grease the insides of nine 3×1⅝-inch pastry rings and place them on top of the baking sheet.

. . . .

To make "collars" for the tarts, cut another piece of parchment paper or waxed paper into nine 11×3½-inch strips. Grease both sides of the strips and line each ring with a strip. The collar should extend beyond the height of the ring to accommodate the rise of the meringue.

. . . .

In a double boiler over simmering water, combine the chocolate, butter, and cocoa. Stir until the ingredients have melted and are well blended. Set aside.

. . . .

Separate the eggs, placing the yolks in a medium bowl and the whites in a large bowl.

. . . .

Using an electric mixer set at medium speed, beat the egg whites until they form soft peaks. Increase speed to medium-high and gradually add the sugar. Continue to beat until stiff, glossy peaks form.

. . . .

Add the hot espresso to the chocolate mixture and stir with a wire whisk until blended. Add the egg yolks, all at once, and whisk briskly until all the ingredients are well combined. Stir in one-third of the meringue to soften the chocolate. Gently fold the chocolate mixture into the remaining whites until well blended.

. . . .

Pour a ⅓-inch-thick layer of the chocolate meringue into each of the prepared pastry rings. Set the remaining chocolate meringue aside.

. . . .

Bake in the oven for 5 minutes. Transfer to a wire rack to cool. Once the tart bottoms have reached room temperature, evenly distribute the remaining chocolate meringue among the rings (there should be about 2 inches of batter in each ring).

. . . .

Bake the tarts in the oven for 6 to 7 minutes. The inside of the tarts should remain moist and runny while the tops are slightly firm to the touch. Using a metal spatula, gently transfer the tarts to individual dessert plates. Remove the rings and the parchment paper. Serve immediately.

Editor's note: This recipe also freezes well. Follow the directions for precooking the tart bottoms and filling the rings with meringue, then place in the freezer. About 30 minutes before serving, preheat the oven to 375 degrees F. Remove the pan from the freezer and let the tarts defrost for 5 minutes. Bake for 7 to 8 minutes. Remove the tarts from the oven and serve.

HOT TARTS WITH BITTER CHOCOLATE

5½ ounces extra-bitter chocolate, preferably Valrhona, chopped

½ cup (1 stick) plus 1½ teaspoons unsalted butter, cut into pieces

¼ cup unsweetened cocoa powder

5 large eggs

¾ cup plus 2 tablespoons sugar

¼ cup hot brewed espresso

SERVES

9

Sonia Rykiel

RECIPE PHOTOGRAPH ON PAGE 152

preparation

In a double boiler over simmering water, melt the chocolate. Whisk in the butter until it has melted and the mixture is smooth. Remove from heat and whisk in the egg yolks and zest until blended. Set aside.

....

In a large bowl, using an electric mixer set at medium speed, beat the egg whites until soft peaks form. Add the sugar 1 tablespoon at a time and continue to beat until the sugar has dissolved and the whites form stiff, glossy peaks.

....

Remove the top portion of the double boiler from the hot water portion. Using a rubber spatula, stir one-third of the egg white mixture into the chocolate. Pour this mixture into the remaining egg whites and gently fold until well blended.

....

Carefully spoon the mousse into 6 individual serving bowls, glasses, or ramekins, and refrigerate until chilled.

CHOCOLATE MOUSSE

9 ounces dark chocolate, chopped

½ cup (1 stick) unsalted butter

3 large egg yolks, lightly beaten

Grated zest of 1 orange

6 large egg whites

4 tablespoons sugar

SERVES

6

SINCE I WAS A LITTLE GIRL, I HAVE

LOVED CHOCOLATE. IT IS AS IF I WERE

SURROUNDED BY BOUCHÉES DE GANACHE,

ROCHERS PRALINÉS, TARTS STUFFED WITH

CREAM, AND CHOCOLATE BARS.

I HAVE NEVER BEEN ABLE TO DO

WITHOUT CHOCOLATE, PARTICULARLY,

CHOCOLATE MOUSSE, MY MAD PASSION.

The Honorable & Mrs James R. Thompson

preparation

Preheat the oven to 375 degrees F. In a large bowl, using an electric mixer set at the lowest speed, combine the flour, ½ cup of the granulated sugar, and all the remaining ingredients except the kisses, until well blended. Scoop out 1 tablespoon-sized portions of the dough and roll them between your palms into 1-inch-diameter balls.

• • • • • • • • • • • • • • • •

Pour the remaining ¼ cup sugar on a small plate. Roll the dough balls in the sugar until they are completely coated. Place the balls 2½ inches apart on an ungreased baking sheet. Repeat until all the dough has been used.

• • • • • • • • • • • • • • • •

Bake in the oven for 10 to 12 minutes, or until the tops begin to crack. Remove the baking sheets from the oven. Quickly place a chocolate kiss flat side down in the center of each cookie, pressing down firmly so that the cookie cracks around the edges. Transfer the cookies to a rack to cool completely.

When I was a little girl growing up in the 1950s, I loved to regale my mother with stories of all the exciting things I would do when I grew up and became a lawyer. She always listened to me and encouraged me in my education, but she also always ended these conversations with the same advice: "Learn another recipe, dear." I followed my dream and became a lawyer, but I also took my mother's advice and learned all of her recipes, including this one for peanut butter kisses. To this day, I meet people who remember this cookie from their own childhood with great fondness. For them, and for me, it triggers warm feelings of love and home.

PEANUT BUTTER KISSES

1¾ cups unbleached all-purpose flour

¾ cup granulated sugar

½ cup firmly packed brown sugar

½ cup (1 stick) unsalted butter at room temperature

½ cup creamy peanut butter

1 large egg

2 tablespoons milk

1 teaspoon baking soda

½ teaspoon salt

1 teaspoon vanilla extract

48 milk-chocolate candy kisses

MAKES

48

Merci bien...
THANK YOU ...

Yves Thuries

preparation

Line a baking sheet with parchment paper or waxed paper and top with twelve 4×½-inch pastry rings.

· · · · · · · · · · · · ·

In a small saucepan, bring the lemon juice and heavy cream to a boil over medium-high heat.

· · · · · · · · · · · · ·

Meanwhile, in a medium saucepan, mix together the egg yolks, ¼ cup of the granulated sugar, and the cornstarch. Pour the boiling lemon mixture into the egg yolk mixture. Stir and bring back to a boil over medium-high heat. Cook for 5 minutes, stirring constantly with a wooden spoon. Set aside.

· · · · · · · · · · · · ·

In a small bowl, combine the gelatin and ½ cup of the cold water. Stir and let stand for 1 minute. Add the ½ cup hot water and stir until the gelatin has dissolved. Add the gelatin to the egg yolk mixture and stir until well combined. Set aside.

· · · · · · · · · · · · ·

In a large bowl, using an electric mixer set at medium-high speed, beat the egg whites and the 1 tablespoon sugar until soft peaks form.

· · · · · · · · · · · · ·

In a small saucepan, combine the remaining 1½ cups of sugar and the remaining ½ cup cold water. Bring to a boil over high heat. Continue to boil until the temperature reaches 248 degrees F on a candy thermometer, or when a bit of syrup, immersed in cold water, forms a soft ball between the fingertips.

Remove from heat. Set the electric mixer at the highest speed and continue beating the egg whites while gradually adding the sugar syrup. Be careful to pour the syrup against the side of the bowl; do not let the syrup hit the beater or it will spray and harden. Beat for 2 to 3 minutes, or until stiff, glossy peaks form. Reduce the speed to low and add the hot lemon cream mixture. Mix well.

· · · · · · · · · · · · ·

Fill a pastry bag with this mixture, and pipe it into the bottom third of the rings. Arrange a layer of raspberries on top. Fill with additional lemon mixture. Use a straight spatula or dinner knife to level off the top of each circle. Place the baking sheet in the refrigerator for 3 hours.

· · · · · · · · · · · · ·

To make the raspberry coulis, place the raspberries, confectioners' sugar, and lemon juice in a food processor fitted with a steel blade, or a blender. Process for 20 seconds, or until well blended. Strain the mixture through a fine-meshed sieve into a bowl.

· · · · · · · · · · · · ·

Preheat the broiler. Sprinkle the gratins with confectioners' sugar, and place 6 inches under the broiler for about 30 to 45 seconds, or until lightly golden. Be careful not to burn them.

· · · · · · · · · · · · ·

Place the gratins on individual dessert plates. Spoon the raspberry coulis around the gratins and serve immediately.

GRATINS OF RASPBERRIES

Gratins

⅓ cup fresh lemon juice

½ cup heavy cream

5 large eggs, separated

1¾ cups plus 1 tablespoon granulated sugar

2 tablespoons cornstarch

1½ teaspoons plain gelatin

1 cup cold water

½ cup hot water

8 cups fresh white or red raspberries

Raspberry Coulis

8 cups fresh red raspberries

2 tablespoons confectioners' sugar, sifted

¼ cup fresh lemon juice

¼ cup confectioners' sugar, sifted

SERVES

12

Editor's note:
This dessert freezes well.
When ready to serve, preheat
the oven to 375 degrees F.
Remove the gratins
from the freezer, sprinkle
with confectioners' sugar,
and bake for 10 to 12 minutes.

Katie Couric

preparation

Preheat the oven to 350 degrees F. Grease and flour a 9×12-inch baking pan.

. . . .

To make the crust, combine the flour, confectioners' sugar, and a pinch of salt in a medium bowl.
Using a pastry blender or 2 knives, cut in the butter until the mixture is crumbly.
With your fingertips, press the crust mixture evenly into the prepared pan.
Bake in the oven for 20 minutes, or until the crust is golden. Place the pan on a wire rack
to cool, leaving the oven on.

. . . .

To make the filling, place the granulated sugar, flour, eggs, and lemon juice in a medium bowl.
Using an electric mixer set at lowest speed, combine the ingredients for 30 seconds.
Stir in the lemon zest.

. . . .

Pour the filling on top of the baked crust. Bake in the oven for 30 minutes, or until a toothpick
inserted in the center comes out clean. Place on a wire rack to cool.

. . . .

When completely cooled, dust the top lightly with confectioners' sugar.
Cut into 3-inch squares to serve.

*Editor's note: Your family will love these lemony treats as a dessert,
but they are also wonderful with afternoon tea.*

← —— 3 INCHES —— →

CUTTING GUIDE

3 INCHES

LEMON LOVES

Crust

2 cups unbleached all-purpose flour

½ cup confectioners' sugar, sifted

Salt

1 cup (2 sticks) unsalted butter
at room temperature

Filling

2 cups granulated sugar

¼ cup plus 2 tablespoons unbleached
all-purpose flour

4 large eggs

6 tablespoons fresh lemon juice

2 tablespoons finely grated
lemon zest

¼ cup confectioners' sugar, sifted

MAKES TWELVE
3-INCH SQUARES.
SERVES

12

CHRISTINE'S LEMON CAKE

1½ cups unbleached all-purpose flour, sifted

¾ teaspoon baking powder

Grated zest of 2 medium lemons

¾ cup (1½ sticks) plus 1 tablespoon unsalted butter at room temperature

¾ cup plus 1 teaspoon granulated sugar

4 large eggs

Juice of 2 medium lemons (about 6 tablespoons)

Glaze

½ cup confectioners' sugar, sifted

Juice of 1 medium lemon (about 3 tablespoons)

MAKES ONE 8×4-INCH LOAF CAKE. SERVES — **6**

Every Sunday during the winter when it is time for a snack, we meet at our friend Christine's house. She prepares this wonderful lemon cake for friends and children. Even the greatest gourmand fights over the crumbs. Though we've seen her make this cake so many times, ours is never as good. Our friend must have a secret – perhaps you will discover it!

preparation

Preheat the oven to 350 degrees F. Grease and flour an 8×4-inch loaf pan.

. . . .

In a medium bowl, combine the flour, baking powder, and lemon zest. Set aside. In a large bowl, using an electric mixer set at the lowest speed, cream together the butter and granulated sugar until light and fluffy. Continue to blend while alternately adding the dry ingredients (one-fifth at a time), the eggs (one at a time), and the lemon juice (one-fourth at a time), beginning and ending with the dry ingredients. Beat until smooth. Pour the batter into the prepared pan.

. . . .

Bake for 50 minutes, or until a toothpick inserted in the center of the cake comes out clean.

. . . .

To make the glaze, combine the confectioners' sugar and the lemon juice in a small bowl. While the cake is still hot, pour the glaze over the top and spread evenly with a pastry brush. Serve warm or cool.

Pierre

Michel

Gloria Estefan

FLAN

1½ cups plus 1 teaspoon sugar

8 large egg yolks

4 large eggs

One 14-ounce can sweetened
condensed milk

One 12-ounce can evaporated milk

1 cup milk

⅛ teaspoon salt

1 tablespoon vanilla extract

SERVES

10

preparation

Preheat the oven to 300 degrees F. To make the caramel, place the 1½ cups sugar in a small, heavy saucepan. Cook over medium heat, stirring frequently, until the sugar is golden brown. Remove the pan from the heat and immediately pour the caramel into ten 3½×1⅝-inch ramekins, making sure the bottom of each is completely covered. Set aside.

· · · · · · · · · · · · · · · · ·

Using an electric mixer set at the lowest speed, mix the egg yolks and eggs in a large bowl. Beat in the condensed milk, then the evaporated milk, then the regular milk. Using a wire whisk, gently mix in the remaining 1 teaspoon sugar, the salt, and vanilla.

· · · · · · · · · · · · · · · · ·

Slowly pour an equal amount of the custard into each of the ramekins. Using a spoon, skim off any bubbles that form on top. Transfer the ramekins to a baking dish filled with hot water,

making sure the water comes two-thirds the way up the sides of the ramekins. Bake in the oven for 1 hour or until the centers of the flans are firm to the touch.

· · · · · · · · · · · · · · · · ·

Place each ramekin on a wire rack to cool for 10 minutes. Refrigerate to cool completely, at least 3 hours.

· · · · · · · · · · · · · · · · ·

To unmold, run a sharp knife very carefully around the edge of the custard. Place a dessert plate on top, flip it over, and tap gently until the flan is loose. Remove the ramekin.

· · · · · · · · · · · · · · · · ·

Serve slightly chilled or at room temperature.

Editor's note: This rich, creamy custard is a perfect ending to a spicy Southwestern, Mexican, or Cuban meal.

Clint Black &
Lisa Hartman Black

preparation

Combine all the ingredients in a blender.

Blend on the highest speed until smooth.

· · · · · · · · · · · ·

Serve immediately in a tall frosted glass.

SKINNY
CHOCOLATE
BANANA

1 cup ice cubes

4 heaping teaspoons sugar-free
instant cocoa

½ cup nonfat milk

½ cup brewed decaffeinated coffee
at room temperature

1 banana

1 packet sugar substitute (optional)

SERVES

1

One *night* we had a
serious *sweet* tooth,
but didn't want to give in
to a box of *cookies*.
So we decided to create
our own *sweet satisfier*.
And this is what we created.

Austin O'Brien

par-tion

Combine all the ingredients in a blender.
Blend on the highest speed until smooth.

Serve immediately in tall frosted glasses.

I LEARNED TO MAKE SMOOTHIES
ON THE SET OF LAST **ACTION** HERO
FROM MIKE KEHOE. I EXPERIMENT
A LOT. TRY IT WITH DIFFERENT JUICES
OR FRUIT. IT'S FUN, NOT TO MENTION
DELICIOUS AND HEALTHY!

LAST ACTION SMOOTHIE

1 cup ice

1 cup cranberry juice

One 6-ounce container
mixed-berry yogurt

2 cups frozen strawberries

3 bananas, cut in thirds

SERVES

4

WARM LIQUID-CENTER BITTERSWEET CHOCOLATE CAKE WITH BERRY AND PASSION FRUIT SAUCE

═══════

Chocolate Genoise
¼ cup unbleached all-purpose flour
¼ cup unsweetened cocoa powder
4 large eggs
½ cup sugar
Cake Batter
4 ounces bittersweet chocolate
1 large egg
4 tablespoons sugar
2½ tablespoons sourdough starter
½ cup (about 4) egg whites
Chocolate Ganache
4½ ounces bittersweet
chocolate, chopped
1½ teaspoons unsalted butter
½ cup heavy cream
1½ teaspoons sugar
Berry and Passion Fruit Sauce
¼ cup plus 1 tablespoon sugar
¼ cup plus 1 tablespoon water
3 tablespoons passion fruit pulp
(fresh or frozen)
12 fresh blueberries, halved
6 large fresh blackberries,
cut into thirds
30 fresh raspberries
24 fresh red or black currants
18 slices kiwi fruit, ⅛-inch thick

SERVES

6

Chocolate is my favorite way to end a meal,

and this particular preparation is so intense

it almost makes your head buzz.

With the liquid center and the delicate

soufflé-like cake, the juxtaposition of textures

and flavors makes for great complexity.

A little delicate fruit sauce adds an acidic foil

to the intense chocolate, and it could be taken

a step further by adding ice cream or sorbet

to the plate.

Charlie Trotter

preparation

Preheat the oven to 350 degrees F. Grease a 15½×10½-inch sided baking sheet. Line the baking sheet with parchment paper, grease the paper, and flour it very lightly.

. . . .

To make the chocolate genoise, sift the flour and cocoa together into a small bowl. Set aside. In a medium saucepan, whisk the eggs and sugar together. Place over medium heat and warm to 110 degrees F, or until the mixture has a ribbon-like consistency. Transfer the egg mixture to a large bowl. Using an electric mixer set at medium-high speed, beat the mixture until it triples in volume. Quickly but gently fold in the flour and cocoa. Spread the batter evenly onto the prepared pan. Bake in the oven for 5 minutes.

. . . .

Loosen the sides of the genoise with a knife and immediately turn the genoise out onto a pastry cloth. Using a pastry ring, cut out six 3-inch circles and set the circles aside.

. . . .

To make the cake batter, melt the chocolate in a double boiler over simmering water. In a small bowl, whisk together the egg and 2 tablespoons of the sugar until the mixture is pale in color. Place the sourdough starter in a medium bowl. Fold in the egg mixture, then the melted chocolate. Cover and refrigerate until ready to use.

. . . .

In a large bowl, using an electric mixer set at medium speed, beat the egg whites until soft peaks form. Increase the speed to medium-high, and gradually add the remaining 2 tablespoons sugar. Continue to beat until stiff, glossy peaks form. Carefully fold the meringue into the chocolate mixture.

. . . .

To make the chocolate ganache, place the chopped chocolate in a medium bowl with the butter. In a small saucepan, combine the cream and sugar. Place over medium-high heat and bring to a boil. Remove from heat and immediately whisk the cream into the chocolate. Continue whisking until the mixture is smooth. Set aside.

. . . .

Preheat the oven to 425 degrees F. Line a 15½×10½-inch sided baking sheet with parchment paper or aluminum foil and grease it.

. . . .

Grease the insides of six 3×1⅝-inch pastry rings, and place them on top of the baking sheet.

. . . .

To assemble, place a genoise circle in the bottom of each of the prepared rings and top with a 1-inch diameter ball of ganache. Spoon or pipe the cake batter around each mound, filling the ring four-fifths full, and completely covering the ganache.

. . . .

Bake in the oven for 5 to 6 minutes, or until slightly firm to the touch. Place the sheet on a wire rack.

. . . .

Meanwhile, to make the sauce, combine the sugar and water in a small saucepan. Bring to a boil over high heat, stirring frequently, until the sugar is dissolved.

. . . .

Whisk the sugar syrup and the passion fruit pulp together in a small bowl. Pass the syrup through a fine-meshed sieve into a small bowl.

. . . .

Place the remaining ingredients in a large saucepan. Pour in half of the passion fruit syrup and gently toss to mix. Warm over medium-low heat.

. . . .

To serve, place a warm cake in the center of each of six individual dessert plates. Divide the fruit among the plates and spoon some of the remaining passion fruit syrup around the cakes. Serve immediately.

THIS IS MY MOTHER'S RECIPE, AND IT IS THE RICHEST, DENSEST CHEESECAKE EVER!

I GREW UP EATING THIS CAKE, LOOKING FORWARD TO BEING OLD ENOUGH

TO MAKE THIS RECIPE FOR MYSELF WHENEVER I WANTED IT.

Elizabeth Glaser

preparation

Preheat the oven to 375 degrees F. Grease the bottom and sides of a 10-inch springform cake pan.

. . . .

To make the crust, place the zwieback toasts into a plastic bag and close. Using a rolling pin, gently roll over the toasts to make crumbs. Combine the zwieback crumbs, sugar, butter, and cinnamon together in a large bowl. Stir to blend. Reserve 3 tablespoons of the mixture. Take three-fourths of the remaining crumbs and press them firmly on the bottom of the cake pan. Press the remaining crumbs three-fourths of the way up the sides.

. . . .

To make the filling, put the cream cheese in a large bowl. Using an electric mixer set at medium speed, gradually add the eggs to the cream cheese. Add the sugar, lemon juice, and salt, and beat until smooth. Pour the filling into the prepared pan. Bake in the oven for 45 minutes.

. . . .

Meanwhile, to make the topping, combine the sour cream, sugar, and vanilla in a medium bowl and stir until smooth. Set aside.

. . . .

After 45 minutes, remove the cake from the oven. At this point the center of the cake will not be firm. Increase the oven temperature to 475 degrees F. Immediately spoon the sour cream mixture on top of the cake. Sprinkle the reserved crumbs evenly across the top. Bake in the oven 15 minutes longer. The cake will still not be totally firm at this point.

. . . .

Let the cake cool on a rack to room temperature, about 1 hour. Refrigerate 6 hours or overnight.

. . . .

Carefully remove the sides of the pan and transfer the cake to a serving plate.
Cut into wedges to serve.

MY MOM'S FAMOUS CHEESECAKE

Crust

4 cups (two 6-ounce boxes) zwieback toast

¼ cup sugar

½ cup (1 stick) unsalted butter, melted

1 teaspoon ground cinnamon

Filling

2 pounds cream cheese at room temperature

4 large eggs

1 cup sugar

1 tablespoon fresh lemon juice

¼ teaspoon salt

Topping

2 cups sour cream

¼ cup sugar

1 teaspoon vanilla extract

MAKES ONE 10-INCH CHEESECAKE.
SERVES

12

tables of conversion

LIQUID WEIGHTS

¼ teaspoon	1.23 ml
½ teaspoon	2.5 ml
¾ teaspoon	3.7 ml
1 teaspoon	5 ml
1 dessertspoon	10 ml
1 tablespoon (3 teaspoons)	15 ml
2 tablespoons (1 ounce)	30 ml
¼ cup	60 ml
⅓ cup	80 ml
½ cup	120 ml
⅔ cup	160 ml
¾ cup	180 ml
1 cup (8 ounces)	240 ml
2 cups (1 pint)	480 ml
3 cups	720 ml
4 cups (1 quart)	1 litre
4 quarts (1 gallon)	3¾ litres

TEMPERATURES

32°F (water freezes)	0°C
200°F	95°C
212°F (water boils)	100°C
250°F	120°C
275°F	135°C
300°F (slow oven)	150°C
325°F	160°C
350°F (moderate oven)	175°C
375°F	190°C
400°F (hot oven)	205°C
425°F	220°C
450°F (very hot oven)	230°C
475°F	245°C
500°F (extremely hot oven)	260°C

DRY WEIGHTS

¼ ounce	7 grams
⅓ ounce	10 grams
½ ounce	14 grams
1 ounce	28 grams
1½ ounces	42 grams
1¾ ounces	50 grams
2 ounces	57 grams
3 ounces	85 grams
3½ ounces	100 grams
4 ounces (¼ pound)	114 grams
6 ounces	170 grams
8 ounces (½ pound)	227 grams
9 ounces	250 grams
16 ounces (1 pound)	464 grams

LENGTH

⅛ inch	3 mm
¼ inch	6 mm
⅜ inch	1 cm
½ inch	1.2 cm
¾ inch	2 cm
1 inch	2.5 cm
1¼ inches	3.1 cm
1½ inches	3.7 cm
2 inches	5 cm
3 inches	7.5 cm
4 inches	10 cm
5 inches	12.5 cm

APPROXIMATE EQUIVALENTS

1 kilo is slightly more than 2 pounds

1 litre is slightly more than 1 quart

1 meter is slightly over 3 feet

1 centimeter is approximately ⅜ inch

mission statements

___

DIFFA is the oldest national funder of AIDS services. Through its broad fund-raising experience, over twenty million dollars have been granted to more than 900 grassroots HIV/AIDS organizations since 1984.

DIFFA/Chicago is the Chicago design industries' response to a national emergency. Through educational and cultural programs, we help Chicago to rally and fight against this fatal disease. We put creative genius to work with cause-related marketing with great events like DIFFA/Chicago's Annual Gala, Designer's Garage Sale and Oak Street's Passport to International Fashion. We return corporate and private dollars to the Chicago community for the care, treatment and education of people living with HIV/AIDS. And we are expanding our grant-making priorities to include populations at risk today: women, African Americans, Latinos and teens.

___

For more information or to make a donation please contact:

DIFFA/CHICAGO

Suite 751, Apparel Center · 350 North Orleans · Chicago IL 60654 · TELEPHONE 312-321-9290

THE PEDIATRIC AIDS FOUNDATION is the only national non-profit foundation identifying, funding, and conducting pediatric AIDS research internationally.

Co-founded by Elizabeth Glaser, Susan DeLaurentis, and Susie Zeegen in 1988, the Pediatric AIDS Foundation's primary objective is to create a future that offers hope through research leading to effective therapies and methods for blocking transmission from infected mothers to newborns.

The Foundation's less than 6% administrative overhead ensures that the highest possible percentage of all dollars raised goes directly to fund basic medical research; emergency assistance, providing funds for unmet needs of children with HIV/AIDS; student intern awards and a national Parent Education Program that stresses knowledge, compassion, and a call to action.

___

For more information please contact:

PEDIATRIC AIDS FOUNDATION

1311 Colorado Avenue · Santa Monica CA 90404 · TELEPHONE 310-395-9051

To make a donation by credit card, please call 1-800-488-5000